FUTURE CITIES
ALL THAT MATTERS

FUTURE
CITIES

CAMILLA WEEN

ALL THAT
MATTERS

ALL THAT
MATTERS

Also available in ebook

'The future is here. It's just not widely distributed yet.'

William Gibson

Contents

Introduction

'A cynic is not merely one who reads bitter lessons from the past; he is one who is prematurely disappointed in the future.'

Sidney J. Harris

The idea of a world of 10 billion people, most of whom will be living in rapidly expanding cities, can be a terrifying prospect. Add to that the effects of climate change and the scarcity of water, energy and food, and it sounds like a bleak future. Without innovation and human ingenuity it might be, but necessity is the mother of invention and *Homo sapiens* is a resourceful species. This book sets out to explain the issues that will face rapidly growing cities in the next 20 to 30 years and how, building on sustainable practices already being introduced around the world, cities can and will grow and flourish. Life could, in fact, be infinitely better than now, although this will necessitate a paradigm shift in our behaviour and attitude towards the environment. The emphasis will be on a move away from the high energy-based practices of the developed world to greener lifestyles, based on sustainable built environments, transport and consumption. Provided there is strong leadership – both from the top in terms of governance and at the bottom within communities – this transition can be achieved over the next couple of decades. The future is bright if you believe in our ability to innovate and succeed.

Population growth

In the era of the first Egyptian dynasty (3000 BCE), the world's population was about 100 million. Over the next 3,000 years it grew to about 250 million by the height of the Roman empire, and less than 2,000 years after that global population hit its first billion in about 1800.[1] Within just over 200 years, in October 2011, the population passed the 7 billion mark and by 2050 it is expected to rise to over 9 billion.

Global population and demography is changing at an alarming rate. The United Nations (UN) now predicts that the global population will reach 10.1 billion by 2100,[2] at which point it will start to plateau. This may appear to be an disturbing figure, but the rate of population growth has actually been falling for the last 40 years. Many of the 10 billion will not be 'new' people, but simply older people, as people are living longer than at any time in the past and life expectancy is likely to continue to rise.

There are plenty of reasons to be optimistic. For example, in the next 25 years the birth rate is expected to fall by about a third – in Istanbul it is already lower than it is in London – and the annual growth rate will be halved from its level at the end of the last century. Professor Danny Dorling, author of *Population 10 Billion*,[3] does not see the current population explosion as a threat, but rather as something that simply happens in nature; he describes it as an 'an algae bloom of human beings'.

Migration to cities

Along with a growing global population, we are also witnessing a dramatic growth in the number and size of cities worldwide. <u>We can't stop urbanization; people move to the city in the expectation of improving their lives.</u> The world is currently in an unprecedented period of urbanization since the earliest cities were established over 9,000 years ago; it is thought that we are currently about halfway through what might be a 50-year period of exceptional urbanization.

In 1950, there were 83 cities with a population of over a million; by 2007, this number had risen to about 470. Today there are 26 cities with populations of over 10 million.[4] These supercities, which may consist of one or several metropolitan regions, are referred to as <u>megacities (a term used by the UN to refer to a metropolitan area with a population of over 10 million)</u>; cities of 20 million are referred to as metacities. Currently, the megacities house 10% of the world's urban dwellers. The term megalopolis that emerged in the early 1800s has been used with both negative and positive connotations. In the early half of the twentieth century, biologist Patrick Geddes and historian Lewis Mumford both used it as a derogatory term, seeing such cities as symptoms of uncontrolled growth; geographer Jean Gottmann,[5] on the other hand, saw positive personal and material opportunity in large agglomerations, such as the chain of metropolitan areas along the northeast coast of the US.

During the next decade or so the growth of cities will be dramatic and fast and it is predicted that the number of megacities will rise to 37.[6] By 2025 the 37 megacities alone will have a combined population of two thirds of a billion people,[7] there will be 18 cities with a population of over 20 million, eight cities will have exceeded 30 million, and Delhi and Tokyo will have over 40 million each. Many of these cities will have grown from a relatively unstructured base, with little infrastructure or governance in place. Interestingly New York, which was the first city to reach a population of 10 million in the middle of the twentieth century, will have slipped down to be the fifth place by 2015.[8] The change in the balance between urban and rural populations in the next 15 years or so will be greatest in Africa and Asia, with Latin America and Oceania following behind. In North America the change is predicted to be 31% while in Europe it is only expected to change by 5%.[9]

Cities start from villages, grow into small towns and eventually become cities. As they grow the boundaries merge together, ultimately forming large megalopolises – vast urban agglomerations or contiguous cities that merge into one and are typically polycentric, having many centres. These will be commonplace in the next 15–20 years. Some megacities are now being thought of as trans-national units, such as the BESETO urban corridor linking Beijing, Pyongyang, Seoul and Tokyo. In the USA the Eastern Seaboard from Washington to Boston could become such a zone.

The World Health Organization (WHO) predicts that the global balance between people living in rural areas and urban areas will shift from the current 50–50 split to 60% living in cities by 2030, and 70% by 2050.[10] In some countries the urban population will be 100%; Singapore has already reached this classification. WHO predicts that urban populations (as opposed to overall population) are set to double by the middle of the twenty-first century from 3.4 billion to 6.4 billion, with most of the growth happening in developing countries.

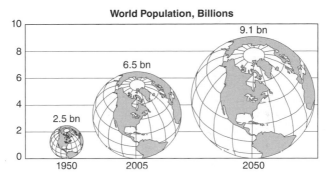

World Population, Billions

▲ The world's population will continue to grow until the middle of the 21st century

The implications of growth

Cities can be thought of as sophisticated machines that support large populations living in close proximity. As a city's population grows, the need for systems to move people and goods, deliver power and water and remove waste, together with institutions to support civic life become critical to its well-being. The challenges of expanding the existing systems or providing new systems, where few or none currently exist, and in a relatively short period of time, are going to be difficult. But cities are not just about functionality; a liveable city must be humane and must offer a decent quality of life for all its inhabitants.

Delivering potentially in a decade a further 10 megacities and hundreds of cities with populations over a million that are pleasant, attractive and well functioning is probably the biggest challenge society has faced since humankind conceived urban living. This book explores the issues and challenges facing cities over the next 20 years and beyond. It looks particularly at the large and very large cities (cities of a few million people to megacities) and their potential evolution over the next 20 to 30 years and beyond.

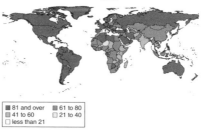

▲ Percentage of world population in urban areas

Many cities will be growing fast, but they will start with differing levels of infrastructure and governance structures, so the challenges they will face will vary. Growing cities fall roughly into three categories, referred to as emerging, transition and mature cities. The emerging cities are characterized as fast growing and likely to double in size within 20 years, as having young populations that have migrated from rural communities with low skills and educational bases. Transition cities will grow less quickly and will typically have established structures so they will be more able to cope with growth; however, they will be experiencing the first signs of an ageing population and will need to meet high demand for infrastructure and services. Mature cities will grow more slowly, or may even shrink, and will have an older population profile; they will have established infrastructure though it will need renewal or upgrading.

The level and rate of change over the last half-century has varied from country to country. For example, the Chinese government has declared it intends to move 250 million people from their rural communities to newly built cities within a little over a decade;[11] this is roughly equivalent to doubling the current 26 largest cities in the world. China has already seen rapid urbanization; in 1950 13% of the population lived in cities, increasing to 40% by 2005, and this is now expected to rise to 60% by 2030. However, in the UK the growth will be from an already higher percentage of urban dwellers; in 1950 79% of the population lived in cities and this is predicted to rise to 92% by 2030, clearly a different scale of change from that of China, and the UK already has a higher proportion of urban dwellers than China is projected to have in 2030. The doom- and gloom-mongers should take note of this; countries can balance growth and maintain concentrations of their populations in cities and still retain natural and rural environments.

The challenges facing rapidly growing cities will be huge. Large cities require complex urban systems and sophisticated infrastructure: water and sewerage, power, transport, as well as social infrastructure such as housing, schools, hospitals, prisons and so on. The planning of infrastructure will be centre stage, equally for high- and low-income countries. The demand for these services is directly related to the population they serve. Major infrastructure projects regularly take 10–15 years to develop and deliver, but we are likely to see many cities double in size in the next decade alone. When governments and consultants want to speed up infrastructure delivery, they generally rely on using tried and tested technologies, but these are coming under increasing scrutiny when viewed against the expectation to meet climate change mitigation targets.

The pressure to find quick solutions to infrastructure delivery will place huge challenges on political decision-makers and funding agencies. There is a tension between those who believe in finding cleaner technologies that use renewable or clean energy and work with nature, and those who believe that technological solutions to deal with the high levels of carbon produced by conventional processes are the answer. As the emerging green alternatives are not yet tried and tested and are often initially more expensive, there will be pressure on some cities with urgent needs to opt for the old and proven systems, while leaving the carbon issue for others to fix.

The provision of housing is obviously central to underpinning a city's well-being, and particularly the supply of decent affordable housing. There are many factors that affect the housing market. On the supply side it is particularly issues of demand, land values, access to funding and/or grants and land use policy (which will include development density), but the flip side is that if a city has a high population on very low incomes then delivering affordable homes is going to be a challenge. If the supply of housing does not meet demand informal settlements will develop within or on the edge of fast-growing cities. Informal settlements, by definition, are not supported by infrastructure, which often leads to poor health and life expectancy within these communities, and the lack of proper roads and transportation means that access to jobs and opportunities is restricted. The way out of poverty becomes increasingly difficult and social problems typically arise.

All change comes at a cost, both social and economic, both of which are likely to be difficult for society to embrace. How cities and nations choose to accommodate the growth will involve social and technological revolutions as well as behaviour adaptation to avoid a spiral into poverty and unrest. This books has set out to capture some of the many examples of how cities have tackled the challenges in innovative ways.

The Big Issues

'Insanity is doing the same thing over and over again and expecting different results.'

Albert Einstein

The key issues

There are two fundamental issues surrounding cities. One is the growth of the world population that is rapidly migrating from the countryside to cities. The second is that cities are massive consumers of energy and 70% of the world's greenhouse gas emissions arise from them.

The scale of growth will be rapid, with many cities doubling in size in the next decade. The UN estimates the present global urban population levels at 3.2 billion and that this will rise to 5 billion by 2030. Poverty and unemployment will be some of the key challenges; by 2030 over 2 billion people are expected to be living in slums.

If city growth is uncontrolled then future prospects for many urban dwellers will be dire. There will be increasing stress on infrastructure, which is likely to lead to shortages of water, power and services in the short term, until adequate infrastructure is in place and populations stabilize. For many the quality of life will initially deteriorate. Without adequate planning, the urban infrastructure and social institutions and services, such as education and healthcare, will struggle to cope. Prison populations are likely to grow, stretching already overburdened penal infrastructure. Providing sufficient food will be an ever-increasing problem, with competing demand for scarce resources at the local level, between cities, and worldwide. Transport systems and roads will be highly congested. Unless there is a drastic change in practices, pollution will increase and air quality will deteriorate. To plan for growth, it is necessary to understand which systems will be under most stress.

It is also important to comprehend the consequences of taking no action, i.e. carrying on 'business as usual'.

Cities are complex mixes of technical and social systems – population, economy, employment, products and services – and these interface with transport and communications. This is often referred to as the urban DNA. Understanding this DNA, and the variables of population, housing, public services, economy, demand and capacity helps to project the future action required and its impact on the environment. This is often modelled using computer analysis to best predict priorities and the inter-relationships between variables. This methodology is used extensively in mature cities and when development projects are being funded by government or financial institutions. However, many cities are likely to grow without the benefit of scientific analysis and intuition is likely to be the driver of decision-making. These cities will require help to make smart strategic choices about priorities.

One of the greatest threats to humankind is the impact of activity that results in increased carbon dioxide (CO_2) emissions, which will consequently lead to uncontrolled climate change. The anthropogenic production of CO_2 is currently in excess of the earth's ability to absorb it, resulting in a build up of CO_2, which is hastening climate change. This is particularly pertinent to cities, as even though they occupy only 2% of the earth's land surface, the UN estimates that 70% of all greenhouse gas emissions are attributable to cities.[12] It is generally acknowledged that CO_2 emissions must be reduced, and that this issue must be tackled at the global level, through climate change mitigation policies to which all nations agree.

Tackling CO_2 emissions

How we approach reducing CO_2 emissions depends very much on how we view our relationship with the earth, its biosphere and resources. Broadly there are two camps: those who believe that civilization is a process of conquering the obstacles with clever engineering, and those who believe that the only way to live successfully on our planet is to work in harmony with nature. The 'conquerors' believe that we should not constrain our behaviour or consumption of raw materials, that the earth's resources are there to be taken to support our activity. They assert that the problems of CO_2 emissions and resulting climate change can be engineered away.

Some scientists believe that the problems of increased urbanization and human activity can be fixed by manipulating the earth's natural equilibrium. The logic is that advances in engineering over the last 250 years have made human advancement possible; therefore, the problem that has been created must also have a technical fix. Others believe that since it may be too late to reverse global warming a 'Plan B', consisting of technical solutions, is therefore required to deal with the problems. This techno-scientific approach has been named geo-engineering, defined by the Royal Society as 'the deliberate large-scale manipulation of the planetary environment to counteract anthropogenic climate change'.

Many ideas for geo-engineering solutions are being floated, several fanciful and probably unrealistic. Those now being discussed in some institutions include the removal of carbon from the atmosphere by fertilizing the oceans to encourage phytoplankton, which will, in turn, absorb CO_2 from the atmosphere. Solar radiation management (or solar geo-engineering) to reduce warming is another, which would either reduce solar radiation coming in or reflect it back out into space. One idea is to launch 10 trillion 60-cm reflective discs into space to deflect the sun's rays; another is to create shields of extra bright low-altitude clouds over the oceans. Other strategies focus on capturing the carbon from burning fossil fuels; the thinking is that if it can be captured and stored, then we can carry on burning fossil fuels until they run out, without any worry.

There are many questions surrounding geo-engineering projects, including who is driving this approach and do they have an ulterior commercial motive? Who are the paymasters funding this research? Who ultimately has the authority to make decisions over such planetary interventions? The problem with manipulating the earth's ecosystem is the uncertainty of the outcome. Though we probably understand only a fraction of how it works, we do know that our planet's bio-systems are deeply integrated and in delicate balance; changing one thing could have a catastrophic and quite possibly irreversible impact. Is this a risk worth taking?

Those who believe in the 'harmony with nature' approach see geo-engineering as a doomsday scenario and believe that the solution lies instead in changing the way we live, finding passive solutions to our problems and making do with less. Assuming that the consensus rests on reducing CO_2, then there will be great pressure to develop sustainable solutions for city growth. If the anthropocene era is to have a long healthy future, humans need to be respectful of the earth's ecosystems, rather than trying to find ways to cancel out irresponsible behaviour. Understanding these issues is fundamental to unlocking future good practice for cities. We need a paradigm shift; carrying on business as usual is simply no longer an option. If we are willing to accept a wide range of small-scale changes that would add up to make a big difference, then there is plenty of hope for the future.

Infrastructure delivery

Cities cannot function without infrastructure. The various systems that make the city work are inexorably linked, so their delivery needs to be conceived holistically. This requires strategic planning so that all systems achieve maximum efficiency; for example, conventional sewage treatment is energy demanding, but by switching to anaerobic digestion the process can also become a source of energy. Delivering critical infrastructure is complex and the planning and construction is long and expensive. In parallel, cities will have to reduce their carbon emissions. Cities will have to develop strategies that prioritize the delivery of infrastructure and set clear sustainability targets.

Water and sanitation

Clean water is fundamental to supporting life. The Millennium Development Goals have identified access to safe drinking water and sanitation as a priority. Shortage of drinkable water is a threat to life itself and a city without access to clean water cannot survive. Water and sanitation infrastructure will, arguably, be the most pressing issue for those emerging cities that currently have little infrastructure and particularly if they are in water-scarce parts of the world. Fast delivery of major water infrastructure projects will be a huge challenge in terms of agreements, timescales and funding. A report from WHO and UNICEF[13] has highlighted that the rate of access to clean water and sanitation is not keeping up with population growth.

As cities grow and expand their water needs, there will be growing competition for water between neighbouring cities. Rivers and underground aquifers that can support several average cities today will increasingly come under stress as water demand increases. Where scarce water is shared between cities or nations, strategies and agreements will have to be brokered quickly; without water security the potential of civil unrest and disease is high.

Most of our water is extracted from aquifers, which are underground lakes. These aquifers are being drained at an alarming rate and can take hundreds or even thousands of years to replenish. The great Ogallala underground aquifer in the US High Plains is being drained 100 times faster than it is being replenished, with the ground water disappearing in many areas. Similarly, the Hebei Plain aquifer that supplies Beijing is being drained at about twice its natural capacity and Abu Dhabi is expected to have used up its underground water by 2040. Water is also being extracted from the great world rivers at an alarming rate with consequent habitat and species losses.

Where water comes from and how it is shared is a complex question. Those furthest upstream on a river may feel it is their right to use all they need, regardless of those further downstream, and then there is the issue that most of the rain may fall in one country, but collect in aquifers that are in another country. This is the case with Palestine and Israel; the Palestinians claim 85% of the local rain falls on their territory, but the water drains to aquifers inside Israel, which extracts 80% of the water for its use.

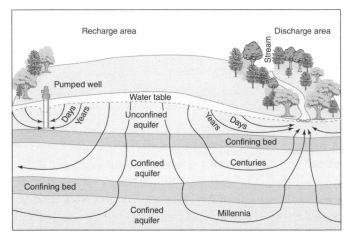

▲ Diagram showing ground source water and the natural speed of replenishment of aquifers

International agreements have been developed to deal with these issues: the *Helsinki Rules on the Uses of the Waters of International Rivers* in 1966, the *UN Convention on the Law of the Non-Navigational Uses of International Watercourses* in 1997, the *Berlin Rules on Water Resources* in 2004. Water equity policy and agreements are still evolving; in 2010, through *Resolution 64/292*, the UN General Assembly explicitly recognized the human right to water and sanitation and acknowledged that these are essential to the realization of all human rights. Though there is plenty of legislation to prevent inequitable practice and abuse of water, the reality is that the best results are achieved through collaboration, mutual understanding and respect.

Resources, waste and recycling

We know almost everything we do now could be done more efficiently; that means improved and innovative technology. We can reduce much waste simply by not producing it in the first place and we need to consider the future re-use of manufactured goods and raw materials, the capture of by-products and the re-use of much of what we currently throw away. The solutions have to lie in switching to more renewable resources and away from exhaustible resources. There will be a growing need for robust agreements to be negotiated about sharing scarce resources between cities, states and the entire planet. Equitable trading of the world's resources will inevitably become a global issue and the question will be whether states will agree, and, if not, whether the UN will be strong enough to broker these agreements.

Cities have traditionally produced vast amounts of waste, which has had to be disposed of. Landfill has been the easy option. Though lack of suitable sites is increasingly becoming a problem, the fundamental issue is that we are throwing away precious resources. We need to develop rigorous processes to re-use, recycle and reduce our waste. Another aspect is the careful disposal of hazardous waste, to prevent contamination of land and (potentially) watercourses. This is an expensive process, and charging for the service is only likely to lead to illegal dumping. Cities will need to weigh up the risks. Probably the best option is a combination of providing the disposal service for free and implementing heavy fines for illegal dumping.

Energy

It is incumbent upon cities to reduce their greenhouse gas emissions by migrating towards renewable or clean energy sources. It is probably also necessary to reduce consumption, but without energy, cities cannot function. Cities need adequate energy to power their infrastructure and to provide for domestic needs. It is vital that countries that are currently low energy consumers, when developing the infrastructure that is necessary to support the expanding populations, do not replicate the carbon-intensive solutions of most of major cities. Low-carbon living will have to be the norm in the future.

Even if the electricity is generated far away, if it comes from fossil fuels, the carbon emissions will nonetheless be contributing to global climate change and there will be a responsibility on cities to reduce this. <u>The big challenge is to move the energy sources away from fossil-based fuels and to make them carbon neutral in a very short space of time</u>.

Housing

Growing cities clearly need to increase their housing stock. The challenges will depend very much on the base starting point. In mature cities, land will be expensive and in short supply and many of these cities' expansion will be controlled by containment boundaries, such as the 'green belt', or by naturally physical barriers. Transition cities may have more flexibility, but land values are likely to be rising fast as developers seize the opportunity for quick profit. Most emerging cities are likely to have grown ad hoc, with little thought to overall future planning or vision. These cities will have to review quickly what has already been established and set out how new housing can be properly delivered and integrated with the existing supply.

Furthermore, all cities will have to ensure a range of housing, particularly affordable housing for low-income groups. In 2013, 863 million people lived in slums, that is a quarter of all urban dwellers.[14] It is predicted that by 2030 there will be 2 billion squatters, rising to 3 billion by 2050. This will mean a third of all people on the planet living in unplanned, illegal and most probably inadequate housing, with no rights or security. In sub-Saharan Africa, 62% of the urban population currently lives in slums; for south-central Asia this figure is 43%. This is a gigantic challenge for cities, now and even more so in the future.

Food

Feeding 7, 8, 9 or 10 billion is a concern. There will be competing demand for food locally, between cities, and worldwide. The estimate is that food production will have to be doubled or even tripled in the next 30-40 years. Many scientists now believe that intensive farming has peaked and the land is thought to have reached its maximum capacity. Currently 50-70% of our food is produced in the developing world; it is likely to be the food producer of the future. There are an estimated 470 million small-scale farms (of 1-2 hectares) across the globe, most of which are in the developing world. The UN is now saying that if we do not support the concept of small-scale farming there will be no food security in the future. Future farming practice will need to be smarter, more sustainable, resilient and supportive of biodiversity and the concept of farming within the city is likely to take hold.

Transport

Good transport and mobility is vital for a well-functioning city and correlates very closely to GDP. However, with growing demand, transport systems and road networks will become highly congested. A big concern for fast-growing cities is going to be providing sufficient capacity without increasing pollution. Transport is currently a significant contributor to greenhouse gas emissions and pollution; in the USA it is responsible for roughly a third of all emissions and worldwide the figure is one fifth.[15] Continued reliance on fossil fuel based vehicles will result in increasing pollution and deteriorating air quality, so there will be pressure to commit to clean options that reduce CO_2 emissions.

Rapidly growing cities will struggle to provide sufficient capacity quickly enough to meet the growing demand for public transport services and highway space. The challenge will be to keep up with the levels of demand and deliver a mix of transport options. If public transport is infrequent or unreliable then car use is inevitably going to be high. Cities will need to develop a range of solutions that include sustainable mass transit as well as providing for walking and cycling. Major transport infrastructure projects take years to plan and build, so fast-to-deliver options will have to be the immediate focus, with quick solutions coming early, while more complex transport infrastructure projects are developed in parallel over a longer period. In mature cities it is likely that the transport issues are primarily about renewal and upgrading of the existing systems and developing ways of making the existing systems more efficient.

Humans love cars and as we develop economically, it is the ultimate aspiration to own a car. The perception is that car travel in cities is fast and convenient, but hours are spent all over the globe every day sitting in traffic jams. Traffic congestion is a disaster for the economy. A UK Government paper in 2008 estimated that rising congestion could waste £22 billion-worth of time every year in England by 2025, and increase costs to business by over £10 billion per year.[16] It is imperative for all cities to shift the emphasis from car travel to public transport, cycling and walking, but this relies on having as the alternative a fast and convenient public transport network. Public transport is a massive investment and it does not pay for itself, so cities will have to subsidise transport; this cannot be avoided, but it is sound investment as good transport is good for business.

Social infrastructure

As urban populations grow, the social services that support those in need of help will become stretched. The western model of healthcare delivery is likely to have to undergo great change, with hospitals, accident and emergency services and therapy clinics needing to find alternative, efficient ways to deliver services. Schools and university facilities are likely to struggle to meet demand, so new ways to deliver education will have to evolve, potentially running classes in shifts with remote video links. Fast-growing emerging cities, where a high proportion of the population is likely to have low levels of education and skills, will have to train and build up a workforce quickly in order to run the city and new businesses. Buildings will need to be more flexible, potentially staying open longer to accommodate several uses.

The root causes of crime are complex, but poverty is inevitably a contributing factor, so tackling social inequality will be an important part of the solution. Having adequate policing in a city comes at a cost, and training police forces will be a challenge. However, there is also a growing recognition that local communities play an important role in managing their environment and they should be supported in taking responsibility for creating safe neighbourhoods by, for example, using good urban design. Prisons are likely to become even more overpopulated, which will require new strategies for incarceration and rehabilitation. The use of CCTV for electronic surveillance is a controversial issue; it has been rapidly introduced in many cities, but mainly by stealth; citizens should be engaged in the decision-making process about the use of this technology.

In cities where the population is growing older, social services will face new challenges. According to WHO, the percentage of the population aged over 60 will double from 11% in 2006 to 22% in 2050.[17] Care for the elderly will become an increasing issue, but it is likely that the 60-year-olds will be looking after their 80- and 90-year-old parents instead of enjoying the leisure-filled retirement dream of the late twentieth century. This will require accommodation that is appropriately designed, with more single-level dwellings, and new homes being designed with ageing in mind, known as lifetime homes. Older people are more likely to have mobility issues, so transport services must be designed so that they are 100% accessible. Providing social activities will also be a growing aspect of care for the elderly, so that they can live out their lives in dignity.

The perception that dense cities are places where pestilence is rife is far from reality. Cities have been at the forefront of health reforms that have vastly improved living standards and life expectancy, which is now higher than in rural areas. However, cities will have to maintain education programmes about healthy lifestyles and diet to stem the rise of urban health problems such as obesity.

Economy and employment

Even if all of the above-mentioned problems can be 'fixed', a city needs to thrive economically so as not to be a financial drain on regional or national resources. Cities will therefore need to develop economies that balance revenue and expenditure. The demands on a city's capital expenditure could easily be almost unlimited as we aspire to better and better, but the expenditure can be reduced by improving efficiency, reducing waste and re-using goods and materials. Healthy business communities can be thought of as ecosystems, where different trades and services support and feed each other; cities should aim to create these virtuous circles of production.

Air quality

Poor air quality is an (almost) invisible killer. The United Nations Environment Programme estimates that more than 1 billion people are exposed to outdoor air pollution annually, which is linked to premature deaths. Fine particulates in the air are inhaled and can cause serious lung problems. In cities in developing countries over

90% of air pollution is attributed to vehicle emissions, mainly from older vehicles, poor vehicle maintenance and low fuel quality; measures to reduce vehicle emissions that are now in place in developed countries are lacking in these cities. In the developed world, the increase in diesel vehicles is mainly responsible; these vehicles are good in terms of CO_2 but very bad in terms of particulates. London has attempted to tackle this by creating a Low Emission Zone across the whole of the city, but despite this, London is one of the dirtiest cities in Europe according to a study of 2011[18] and over 4,000 deaths in 2008 were attributed to the effects of poor air.[19] Los Angeles and Phoenix are among the worst in terms of air quality in the USA. Most cities will need to address pollution, particularly from diesel vehicles, as a matter of urgency.

Resilience

Climate change will increase the frequency of storms and floods as well as drought. Cities in vulnerable areas will have to build up their resilience to these types of events, and all cities need to have disaster and recovery plans for unforeseen or unpredictable events, be they earthquakes, fire, volcanic eruption or civil unrest.

Temperatures are expected to rise in most places over the coming decades. The Intergovernmental Panel on Climate Change's *Fifth Assessment Report* (AR5) suggests that there will be a global temperature rise of 1.5–2°C by 2100. In addition to this overall temperature rise, cities suffer from what is referred to as the 'urban heat island' effect. High energy consumption and hard surfaces (which retain solar heat) mean that cities are often 1–3°C warmer than the surrounding countryside. Cities will need to develop strategies to cool themselves naturally by introducing trees and green roofs, exploiting natural prevailing winds and avoiding high-energy air-conditioning systems.

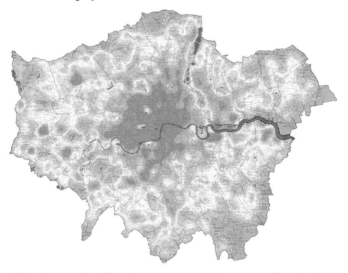

▲ The London Heat Map shows how central London and London's town centres are significantly warmer than the rest of London

The AR5 also predicts that sea levels will rise by 1 m by 2100. This will have very serious implications for low-lying and coastal cities. In many cities the poor occupy the most vulnerable land and their buildings are probably the least resilient. Protecting the millions who live in these zones, or relocating them, has to be a priority that the wider global community needs to address. All vulnerable cities will have to weigh up whether to allow partial inundation or to try to hold the water out. Part of flood defence strategies will have to include setting aside land for flooding so that when storm surges force ocean water inland, the water is diverted away from heavily populated areas. The Netherlands, which has 40% of its land below sea level, is moving away from its traditional practice of keeping water out, and is moving towards a strategy of letting the sea in and adapting its cities to cope with higher water levels; it is creating floating buildings.

London built flood defences in the 1980s to prevent flooding caused by tidal waters flowing up the river Thames. There is little doubt that the threat of flood is increasing: during the 1980s the Thames Barrier was closed four times; during the 1990s it closed 36 times and since 2000 it has had to be closed 100 times.[20]

The complexities of infrastructure delivery

Critical infrastructure projects generally take at least 10 years to deliver (20 years is not unusual), but fast-growing cities will need solutions quickly so there will be temptations to cut corners. At the same time there will be pressure to come up with sustainable solutions, but these will be slower to deliver as the new technologies are still being developed. If the quality of life begins to deteriorate as a result of infrastructure failures, then there will be pressure on politicians to come up with quick fixes. Infrastructure projects are long term and they are often given the go-ahead for political reasons. It has not been unusual to see governments or mayors cancelling projects started by previous administrations. For this reason, the funding of critical infrastructure should be protected from the cycle of politics.

Funding will always be the main hurdle to getting projects off the ground and solutions for securing monies will have to be innovative. Engaging local communities as the innovation and delivery agents can potentially reduce costs, but this will mean new approaches to project management, which is very risk averse; banks and funding agencies need to recognize the value and resourcefulness of local knowledge. Exploring new ways of providing funding and new transaction models needs to happen; something akin to the age-old system of barter might, in some cases, work, with cities trading skills, social capital and resources. Infrastructure projects are perceived as risky and therefore borrowing attracts high interest rates, which often render projects unaffordable. Engaged Investment, a social impact consultancy in London, is gathering evidence to demonstrate that investing in these types of projects is, in reality, not so risky; it hopes to bring about a culture of low-interest loans for urban renewal and expansion projects.

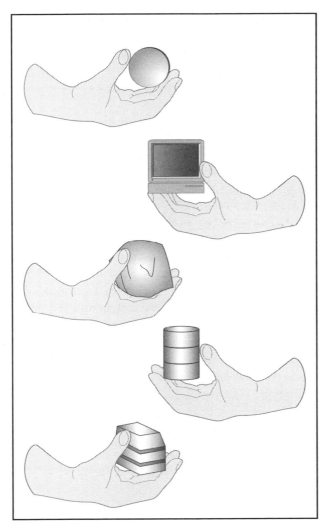

▲ Funding infrastructure projects is likely to be a challenge and new models of exchange will need to be evolved, which include trading social capital

Water Infrastructure

*'We never know the worth of water
till the well is dry.'*

Thomas Fuller

Water is a valuable and renewable resource. If it is used wisely and with a holistic understanding of its virtual presence in so many of our foods and manufactured goods, then there should be enough for all to have sufficient for their needs, both for drinking and for activities. What has to change is the value we place upon it.

Those who suffer most from poor water and sanitation are the urban poor, living in informal settlements. They often have to rely on private vendors for their daily water supply and can pay up to 50 times more for a litre of water than their significantly richer neighbours.[21] Sanitation systems are often completely lacking or inadequate, in the form of open gulleys, and are a serious health hazard. Water resource development is therefore a vitally important aspect of poverty alleviation and economic growth.

Vast amounts of water are used in the developed world for flushing toilets, bathing and general washing. Even more is used in agriculture. Climate change is likely to exacerbate water scarcity and will impact freshwater in three aspects: water quality, water quantity, and water timing, with a change in one often affecting the rest. Water security and water equity is going to be a major concern for the future. Water infrastructure issues will vary widely from grappling with scarcity to making sure that high-quality water is consistently delivered.

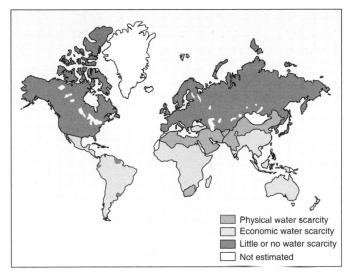

▲ In many parts of both the developed and the developing world, water use is draining water reserves faster than they are being replenished, and this is likely to increase in the future

Sharing water sources

There are currently at least 250 international watercourses in the world shared between two or more sovereign nations; this often leads to tension. As a result managing supply and equitable sharing of water is a challenge and has led to the emergence of integrated approaches to water and environmental management such as Integrated Land and Water Resource Management (ILWRM) and Integrated River Basin Management (IRBM), which presuppose the democratic participation of potentially several political entities or nations. The objectives are to ensure equitable access, agree principles to restrain demand and allocation to industry, agriculture and domestic use, and to restore degraded water and land resources to reduce flood risk and protect ecosystems and heritage, as well as to maximize economic and social benefits. Water-scarce communities will need to develop strong regional agreements so that water is used carefully and equitably, and cities will have to emphasize water conservation and re-use.

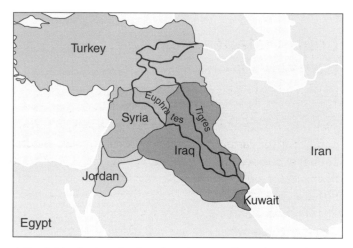

▲ Equitable sharing of water when rivers run through several countries requires democratic agreements. The Tigris and the Euphrates rives are shared by Turkey, Syria and Iraq

The need to reduce demand

Clean water comes at a cost; it is not free and even if there is a plentiful supply, dirty water has to be treated before it can be released back into the environment. The way water is paid for, in many cases indirectly through taxes, fosters a sense that it is 'free'. Having abundant piped water available at the turn of a tap does not encourage water conservation. However, if we have a better understanding of the value of water and the cost of providing it, it should be possible to reduce drastically both demand and wasted water in the developed world. Along with reducing consumption water strategies will need to include water harvesting, water recycling and using grey water, pricing policies and technical restrictions.

Long-distance water transportation

Good-quality water was probably abundant when historic cities were established; it would have been one of the reasons why people settled there. The water may have come from a variety of locations such as groundwater aquifers, surface water lakes and rivers; it might have been conserved water. As historic cities grew, they had to develop solutions to bring in water from outside the cities. The Romans built aqueducts to bring water to Rome, and Constantinople was supplied by a 400 km-long aqueduct completed in the sixth century. Modern cities are now getting their water from further and further away.

In the case of Mexico City, over-extraction of its aquifers has led the city to rely on piping water from the Cutzamala river basin, 150 km away. The Cutzamala transfer system is one of the largest water-supply systems in the world; it has to overcome 1100 m in elevation difference, it includes seven dams and reservoirs for storage, six major pumping stations and a water-purification plant. Increasingly Chinese cities are also relying on water from far away.

The Chinese government is now investing in a massive water-diversion system to move water over hundreds of kilometres from the river Yangtze in the south to farms and cities in northern China, including Beijing. It will take years to complete and is estimated to cost $62 billion.[22]

An alternative to these types of megaproject is to allow innovation to feed into large infrastructure models by opening them up to citizens to conceive new ways of supplying their water needs and including the consumers in the creation of their own water infrastructure. High-energy costs are also associated with water management, as water is heavy, particularly when it has to be pumped over long distances; therefore creating local solutions is sensible.

Tampering with rivers

Long-distance water transfer has relied heavily on dams to create reservoirs, but these are increasingly becoming difficult to deliver. In the last 20 years, the construction of new dams has slowed to a trickle for several reasons, mainly because of the growing costs and greater public environmental awareness that the impact is not just local (where the flooding takes place), but also downstream where ecosystems are often affected. Dams block migratory fish species; they change the natural river flows, which affects the morphology of the riverbeds, floodplains, and coastal deltas. This can in turn increase flood risk, hamper navigation, lower groundwater tables and cause accumulations of toxic materials. Many dams have had dire environmental impacts.

Rivers are also threatened by over-extraction and diversion. For example the river Paraná in South America supplies vast quantities of diverted water for growing sugar cane and coffee and the river Nelson in Canada supplies large quantities of water for growing barley. The river Indus is being heavily depleted by Pakistan for its agriculture and its flows have declined 90% over the last 60 years, which has impacted the Indus dolphin population, with only 100 estimated to be remaining.[23]

Over-extraction

Over-extraction of ground water can also have the consequence of destabilizing ground conditions. Large cities are heavy and if the ground is destabilized then they effectively start to sink; Mexico City has been sinking, which has had negative consequences on its infrastructure. As a result of these types of concern, the city of Shanghai is no longer extracting ground water, but relying on river and reservoir sources.

Desalination

Seawater desalination is a potential source of water, but it comes at a huge cost. It is questionable whether this will ever be a viable source.

Water management

Water management regimes divide water into four 'colour' categories: Blue, which is clean and natural, as it occurs in rivers, lakes, wetlands and aquifers; Green, which is water used to support plant growth; Grey, which is rainwater runoff from buildings and therefore not entirely pure, and Brown, which is sewage and other waste water affected by human activity.

The colour of the water obviously determines its use and value, but it can be improved to a better colour through treatment and filtration processes. Balancing demand and quality to ensure sufficient supply for all uses is the challenge.

Sanitation

In some parts of the world foul water is simply released into rivers, lakes and oceans or it may be re-used for irrigation or industrial use. The environmental implications are obviously unacceptable. Water treatment is, for all cities, a priority infrastructure requirement and potentially one of the largest energy consumers within a city. Cities will, therefore, need to focus on less energy-intensive systems. Anaerobic digestion, which harnesses natural bacteria to break down sewage sludge and other biodegradable materials, is an excellent alternative. Biogas is released during the process, which can then be used as an energy source, thus turning the sewage treatment process from a very energy-hungry operation into a renewable energy producer.

Foul water does have to be transported to the treatment sites, and this will often require extensive infrastructure. Rainwater and surface runoff water also has to be captured to prevent streets and open spaces from flooding.

Two examples of megasewers

Urban sewage systems for megacities will require extensive infrastructure. Mexico City's rapid population growth, from 1.75 million in 1940 to over 21 million today, has put huge stress upon its sanitation system. For hundreds of years the city has manipulated its water, altering hydrology by draining the lakes and rivers and by intensive groundwater extraction. This has caused the city to sink nearly 12 metres in the last 100 years. The waste-water system was extensively damaged by this sinking; 92% of waste water was being discharged untreated into rivers and the metropolitan area produced four times the waste water it had capacity to handle. As a result the city is now building the Túnel Emisor Oriente, scheduled for completion in 2014, which will be one of the largest waste-water tunnels in the world at a cost of over $1 billion.

London's sewage and water-drainage system was built in the Victorian era for a much smaller city. As London has become increasingly built up, the ability of the ground to absorb rainwater has decreased and as a result more goes into the urban drainage system. At times of heavy rain, the water going into the system exceeds the capacity, causing discharge of foul sewage into the river Thames. To address this, the water authority is proposing a megasewer, the Thames Tideway Tunnel, that will run from the west to the east of the city at a projected cost of £4.2 billion. Planning started in 2004 and with a potential completion date of 2023, that will be 19 years, which is not unusual for a megaproject.

Both these examples demonstrate the scale and complexity of sanitation systems likely to be needed in many megacities around the world.

Energy and Waste Infrastructure

'Pollution is nothing but the resources we are not harvesting. We allow them to disperse because we've been ignorant of their value.'

R. Buckminster Fuller

ALL THAT MATTERS

Cities are massive consumers of energy. They are dependent upon electricity for lighting, heating and mechanical services, and, increasingly, for transport. Gas, delivered by gas grids, is also often an essential component of the energy mix. Even with reductions and efficiencies, cities will always be heavily dependent upon energy, particularly in the form of electricity. Decarbonization of energy is the essential big issue in terms of climate change mitigation. The problem with energy infrastructure is that it is expensive, it mostly takes a long time to deliver and it is fraught with political uncertainty as public opinion is very divided over cheap energy or going 'green'. Also the urgent drive to reduce greenhouse gas emissions means that real reductions must be delivered quickly, within the next few years. This will require all countries to sign up to, and adhere to, international agreements. Future energy solutions will have to embrace two parallel strategies; on the one hand reducing consumption and on the other hand finding clean fuel sources and increasing the efficiency of electricity delivery.

Meeting growing demand

As cities grow and new development comes on line, it has to be supplied with electricity. This has traditionally just meant an expansion of the electricity grid network so that it can deliver the extra demand. But power stations have finite capacity and if they are all working at 100% capacity, and the demand is in excess of production, then some areas will experience power cuts. Long-term government plans will be looking at this scenario and thinking about where and when new power plants need to be delivered, and importantly whether these will be traditional fossil-fuelled plants, nuclear or renewable energy plants. Fossil fuel and nuclear power are now under extreme scrutiny by environmentalists; the former for their unarguable greenhouse gas emissions and the latter because of uncertainty around how to dispose of nuclear waste as well as natural or terrorist attack risks. In the developed world in particular, delivery of power infrastructure projects will take many years of debate and argument. The problem is that the two traditional options are both unappealing to the public, whereas the politicians do not believe renewable sources can deliver sufficient to meet all energy demands. The debate around nuclear power is, in many cases, stifling energy policy commitment.

Carbon-free technology

Apart from its artificial cheapness, it is hard to understand why nuclear energy is still being promoted as a viable option. As long as this process generates radioactive waste it will be a highly risky and threatening part of the global infrastructure. The simple truth is that there is no safe way to dispose of nuclear waste; burying it underground is about as safe as setting out to sea in a leaking boat without a life raft. Lead casks, concrete casings or vast underground tunnels like those that are being explored and developed in many countries for nuclear waste storage, are just relying on an insane fantasy that nothing corrodes, that granite rocks have no fissures or clay plugs will never fail, and that water will never permeate through them. The UK has no solution and is storing all its nuclear waste on the surface.

After 70 years of nuclear energy generation there is not one country that has a working final repository for nuclear waste. At some point in the future, there will be radioactive contamination with horrific implications. Even if there was a solution to radioactive waste problem, earthquakes can cause catastrophic damage as was witnessed at the Fukushima nuclear plant in Japan 2011. The USA has two nuclear plants on the Californian fault line. Despite the concerns, many nations are still seeing nuclear as a better energy option than renewable energy.

The alternatives to fossil fuels and nuclear power exist, but are considered by the sceptics to be untested, unreliable and expensive. James Hansen, NASA's chief climatologist, is one such adamant sceptic; he suggests that renewable energies cannot produce sufficient electric power in the foreseeable future.[24] However, The Intergovernmental Panel on Climate Change (IPCC), the international scientific body on climate change, is more sanguine about renewable energy. In its compelling *Special Report on Renewable Energy Source and Climate Change Mitigation*, IPCC scientists concluded in 2011 that 'close to 80% of the world's energy supply could be met by renewables' by 2050, which would cut greenhouse gas emissions by a third.

In many parts of the world electricity grids are already being supplemented by renewable sources such as solar, hydro, and wind power. Following the Fukushima disaster in 2011, Germany took on the nuclear question and in 2012 Chancellor Angela Merkel announced that it would permanently close all nine of its remaining nuclear power plants by 2022 and would introduce renewable technologies. Those opposed predicted blackouts and economic disaster, but there were no blackouts. Rainer Baake, responsible for the plan to phase out nuclear energy, said the critics did not understand that while a single source of renewable energy may not be able to match the constant power of a coal or nuclear plant, a mix of renewable sources can. For example, solar power produces a range of energy during the day, which can be substituted by power from wind, which blows primarily at night. Baake agrees that getting the mix right is not easy, but that Germany's experience does not suggest that it is impossible.

Inefficiencies of conventional electricity

The vast majority of cities get their electricity via a high-voltage grid, with the electricity being generated in power stations far from the city itself. These electrical grids aim to manage the peaks and troughs in demand and on the whole are able to cope pretty well with seasonal demand variations. The UK is covered by a national grid that balances out demand across the whole of the country; if there is a major event on TV, the grid anticipates the commercial break when millions of households go to put the kettle on, which creates a surge in demand. The USA similarly has a nationwide grid. Germany is now talking of a Europe-wide grid. Grids are a web of transmission lines; if a major artery fails then power can be lost to vast areas such as the 2003 blackout in the USA, which affected about 50 million people. The resilience of the grid is therefore of major importance to cities.

Fossil-fuel electricity systems are horrifically inefficient and wasteful; about three quarters of the energy produced is wasted. Of every 100 units of energy within the fossil fuel used to generate electricity, 61 are lost as waste heat, a further 3.5 are lost during transmission and 13 are wasted through inefficient end use. Of those 100 units of energy originally in the fossil fuel, only 22 units actually get used. This cannot be justified when the world is trying to conserve energy and reduce greenhouse gas emissions.[25]

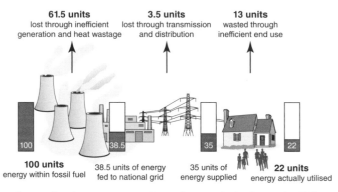

| **61.5 units** lost through inefficient generation and heat wastage | **3.5 units** lost through transmission and distribution | **13 units** wasted through inefficient end use |

| **100 units** energy within fossil fuel | 38.5 units of energy fed to national grid | 35 units of energy supplied | **22 units** energy actually utilised |

▲ Conventional energy generation and transmission is very inefficient

Environmental issues associated with 'clean' hydro generation

Hydroelectric power generation relies on large quantities of water falling to drive turbines that generate the electricity. Though this occurs naturally in a few countries and can be 'tapped', in the majority of cases this is achieved by damming rivers to create large lakes and a vertical drop for the water to fall. This produces cheap clean electricity, and might appear to fit the bill if you are aiming to reduce carbon emissions, but the negative impacts on the environment are much better understood now than they were in the past; building dams has now become highly controversial (the same arguments also apply to creating dams for water reservoirs).

The river Paraná in South America has 29 large dams, mainly for the production of hydroelectricity, which have caused a critical loss of habitat. Akosombo Dam, built in 1963 on the river Volta in Ghana, creating Lake Volta, produces vast quantities of electricity but has also had wide-reaching negative impacts. These include an increase in snail-borne intestinal diseases, the disruption of livelihoods based on river fishing and floodplain agriculture and a dramatic alteration to the ecosystem of the lower river Volta and estuary. In 2006 the Chinese government completed the world's largest dam, the Three Gorges Dam on the river Yangtze. It is 2.2 km long and 184 m tall, over five times as large as the Hoover Dam, and holds back enough water to slow the rotation of the earth. 26 turbines provide 18,000 megawatts of power. However, the environmental and social costs are significant; millions of people have been displaced and arable land, biodiversity and medicinal flora have all been affected.

Moving to carbon-free energy

The huge challenge is to move the energy sources away from fossil fuels and to make them carbon neutral in a very short space of time. Initially, in order to foreground renewable energy alternatives, governments will have to invest and incentivize the switch to green. For example, in Germany house builders and developers are encouraged to look at green energy and there are grants available to investigate whether geothermal energy is an option in a particular area. As a result geothermal energy systems are widely being implemented in Germany, whereas in the UK where this energy form has received virtually no government support it is still relatively rare. Governments will also need to invest in the research and development of all renewable energy sources. Harnessing the vast power locked in the earth's natural systems such as the ocean tides, volcanic activity, hot springs etc. must surely be a priority. Other alternatives, such as fusion energy, are now being developed and tested to understand if they can be viable energy sources, though the problems with transmission and storage still have to be solved.

Fusion power, in contrast to fission power, relies on combining two nuclei, as opposed to splitting one, and the result is heat, which can be harnessed to generate electricity, and there is no radioactive waste. The raw materials are deuterium and tritium, both of which will be abundantly available for millions of years. Scientists believe fusion power is the hope on the horizon; however, according to Professor Steve Cowley of the Culham Centre for Fusion Energy in Oxfordshire, 'The cynics say fusion energy is 30 years away, and always will be.' An abundant source of clean fusion power would have the potential to transform our lives; it would mean clean engines and lower operating costs, which would transform manufacturing and transport. Cowley believes that the big question is not when we can produce electricity this way, but when we will be able to deliver it at an affordable price and in sufficient quantity.[26]

Future practice

As with water and other systems, energy strategies have to include reducing consumption of energy. We will need to be smart about our energy use, capturing waste energy, particularly heat, which is very often a by-product of many processes. There will have to be emphasis on creating energy-efficient machines and buildings, upgrading the energy performance of old buildings, and capturing wasted energy from manufacturing processes as well as all small machines. This will require strong leadership, policies and enforcement, together with incentives for people to carry out upgrades themselves. Planning energy delivery must also focus on ensuring that city systems are integrated to maximize efficiency, and should incentivize innovation.

Waste

▲ The world is running out of landfill sites; waste needs to be re-used, recycled and reduced

Currently most of the world produces literally mountains of waste; the amount is probably roughly proportional to how wealthy a nation is. The developed world has grown up believing that for everything we have finished with now there is a replacement, be it disposable drinking cups, clothes we are bored with, manufactured goods that are last year's model; consumer goods are created to feed this hunger for the 'new'. The trouble is that we are running out of places to put our rubbish, but that is the least of our worries; much of our waste degrades and pollutes the environment and it is an appalling waste of resources and embodied energy just to throw them away. So we have to rethink how we value waste. Like many other things, we need to recognize the value embodied in waste and focus on re-use, recycling materials and capturing energy and resources, instead of dumping. In poor countries most things do have a use; this is actually sustainable practice in action.

We think of waste in terms of the cost of disposing of it. If we start from the perspective that it has value, then we would quickly reduce our waste mountains. The European Union has introduced legislation that restricts the amount of waste that can go to landfill and has an 'End of Life Vehicle Directive' that determines how we deal with our disused cars. This has forced the waste business to rethink its ways. Waste plants are now developing 'closed-loop' systems, which aim to sort, recycle and process everything, and burning only a small amount (that cannot be reused) to generate electricity. These waste plants have the potential to form part of local decentralized energy systems, supplying fuel and also heat that can be used for domestic and commercial heating; thus becoming an integral part of the local economy instead of a financial burden.

Another issue associated with waste is the transport implications of collection from domestic and commercial premises. Our expectation is to have our waste collected from our front doors regularly and frequently, which means that waste collection vehicles have to literally travel up and down each and every street to pick up. An alternative that could be incorporated in new developments is underground vacuum collection; this is explained in Chapter 8.

The biggest opportunity with delivering energy and infrastructure is to identify symbiotic relationships between different activities; what is waste for one process may be fuel for another, such as the example of integrating waste plants with local decentralized energy plants. Planning the different aspects of infrastructure should not be done in isolation, but must be thought of holistically, so that interdependencies can be developed to advantage.

4

Housing

'If you don't think about the future, you cannot have one.'

John Golsworthy

ALL THAT
MATTERS

The *UN Declaration of Human Rights* (Article 25-1) sets out that decent housing is a basic right.[27] It is incumbent upon civilized society to make sure that poor populations who migrate into cities are afforded the opportunity to establish themselves with dignity so that they too can be full citizens of the city. This means that politicians and city administrators must facilitate the establishment of decent communities with the basic human needs.

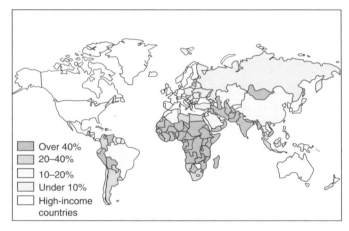

Over 40%
20–40%
10–20%
Under 10%
High-income countries

▲ The UN slum map shows that the concentration of slums is predominantly in developing regions

Slums

Managing housing is a huge challenge for cities. Squatting is occurring widely in many fast-growing cities as rural populations flood into cities and set up whatever makeshift shelter can be cobbled together. These settlements are usually on land not designated for housing development and without formal permission, and are thus illegal. Informal squatter settlement or slum, whatever you call it, it is still home for millions, and it may be the only home they will ever know. Squatters tend to fall outside of political processes and are, to many, invisible. Society has to take responsibility and help them to lead decent and fulfilling lives and ensure that they are properly assimilated into the structure of the city. This responsibility will rest squarely on the shoulders of city administrators; they cannot duck this or wriggle out of it by claiming the settlements are illegal – that is irrelevant.

▲ In cities all over the world, millions of people live in slum settlements. Inadequate as they often are, they do support local communities and these are their homes. The challenge is to find ways to provide necessary infrastructure without destroying the existing social fabric

When people migrate to cities they minimize their housing costs by living in crowded small spaces, often with no sanitation, but the community ties are generally strong. These settlements are perceived as eyesores and this, combined with the illegal activity that tends to flourish, leads city planners to want to remove the settlements entirely. This usually results in the residents being unwillingly evicted from their homes, and although in some cases they are offered alternative housing, the effect is to break up the community ties and their local and informal economy. Eviction rarely works as the settlers will tend to re-group and reform a new slum elsewhere which will probably result in even worse poverty. Forcible displacement and ethnic cleansing (as the slum communities are often made up of a single ethnic immigrant group) is happening regularly right in our midst, in Europe and in democracies, all in the name of regeneration. In the last couple of decades, communities have been forced out of their settlements in Istanbul's Ayazma, Sülemaniye and Sulukule districts, in Lisbon's Fontainhas, in Nairobi, in Mumbai and in many many more cities across the world. The temptation to gentrify historic quarters that have declined is particularly strong and developers know that there is vast profit to be made from shopping malls and luxury housing. But removing someone forcibly from their home is a fundamental human violation.

When urbanization takes place, there is always a bottom band of low-income poor people and they are likely to live in slums. David Smith of the Affordable Housing Institute in Boston suggests that slums are part of the ecosystem of a city. If you think of slums from that perspective they are not so much a threat as a challenge to be sensitively handled. He believes the solutions lie not in removal, but in thinking of ways to improve the physical and social fabric and in facilitating the dwellers to help themselves, so that they can invest their own sweat capital and grow their own wealth. He argues that if you provide the poor with decent affordable housing and, importantly, give them a stake in their homes, then they will make them better and the area is likely to prosper.[28]

Affordable housing

Providing affordable housing for essential city workers, who are often on low incomes, is crucial to ensuring a city has the right workforce mix. This means ensuring that there is an adequate supply of controlled rent properties or access to subsidised mortgage arrangements. If housing is left to developers it is likely to be expensive and targeted at the wealthy. Policies will need to address how housing will be delivered and ensure that there is sufficient affordable housing. There are various mechanisms to ensure this, such as the local government acquiring land early to prevent land values rising uncontrollably. Maintaining affordable housing across the city and not concentrating it in the periphery is also important to avoid the negative implications on transport and infrastructure.

Affordable housing must form part of housing policies. There are various models which focus on different forms of ownership: outright ownership, partial ownership and rental. In some cities the focus is on building housing that is then sold at affordable prices with owners being offered subsidised government mortgages. Partial-ownership models are often developed by social landlords or housing associations, based on the occupier buying a percentage of the value, and may well require subsidy. Affordable rental housing is built and retained either by local authorities or not-for-profit organizations, and rent controls set affordable rents and prevent subletting, which will lead to informal rent escalations. The planning process can also assist the process, by requiring all housing development to deliver a percentage of affordable housing, as has been incorporated in the London Plan.

The local mix of tenants and social groups is a fundamental aspect of creating stable communities. In the UK there have been recent experiments with creating housing schemes with mixed ownership and tenure, referred to as 'blind tenure', where privately owned, interim and low-cost units are seamlessly integrated into the overall design; it is impossible to judge the occupant by where they live. This type of development has been shown to be very successful in fostering strong local communities. Security of tenure for rentees is also a very important aspect of housing, so that occupants can feel secure in their home and can stay as long as they wish.

Density

Density is also a big issue. Dense cities are more efficient and people have shorter distances to travel. The assumption is always that high density equates to high-rise buildings, but low-rise development can also be dense. In fact, the London borough of Kensington and Chelsea has a density of 36,600 people per square mile, which is higher than Kolkata, Lagos or Delhi, but is mainly composed of 6-8 storey buildings.[29]

An interesting diagrammatic representation of city densities can be found on The New York Times website (see 'Manhattan's Population Density, Past and Present', 1 March 2012, www.nytimes.com).

Alternatives to nuclear living

There is a need for housing models to adapt as our social structures evolve. In the developed world the tendency is for more and more people to live alone. This is obviously the most inefficient use of housing stock as two people can live pretty much in the same space as a single person and will share energy and resource-hungry 'white' goods; larger extended families are even more efficient. With the cost of housing likely to keep rising it is probable that housing will get smaller, but also that new models of sharing will evolve. Some of the most pressing needs are for the growing elderly population and how they live, and building design must recognize the needs of the elderly.

Major Infrastructure: Transport

'If I had asked people what they wanted, they would have said faster horses.'

Henry Ford

ALL THAT
MATTERS

The importance of transport

Efficient transport is a fundamental prerequisite for a well-functioning city and is directly related to its economic health, but it is also inexorably linked to greenhouse gas emissions and climate change issues. Cities with good public transport are efficient and generally economically successful. The key to good public transport is to have a mix of macro- and micro-transport modes, including mass transit as well as the finer filigree of walking and cycling networks. All of these should be integrated so that a person can seamlessly and directly change from mode to mode. A city also has to move goods and services, and the efficiency of these systems is also critical to the well-being of the city. Connectivity between cities is also important, as successful local economies will depend on the efficiency of exchange between them, and this connectivity should be developed around rail rather than air and road. The key issues for transport are that it should be environmentally friendly and that it should have sufficient capacity.

Emissions and pollution

Inescapably linked with transport is the issue of greenhouse gas emissions and pollution. The transport sector is responsible for 23% of CO_2 emissions globally and 30% in the Organisation for Economic Co-operation and Development (OECD) area and it is expected to grow by 40% by 2030.[30] The road sector, including freight haulage, is the biggest contributor to emissions and particulates. Public transport systems that rely on electricity may be clean locally, but overall they depend on the process of electricity generation.

Long timescales

Major transport projects have very long timescales, and in democracies the politics and public engagement can add years of delay. In London the process is painfully slow; the Crossrail scheme currently under construction took decades of lobbying, discussion and thwarted parliamentary process to get its parliamentary approval, with a further 10 years of construction.

Future mobility

As cities grow, so does the demand for transport. Future transport solutions will depend on reducing car use, as road space runs out, and public transport services will need to be expanded and freight movement and waste removal rationalized. The working day will potentially have to be lengthened so that work times can be staggered to reduce rush-hour peaks. Measures to encourage higher proportions of walking and cycling journeys will require appropriate infrastructure, such as cycle-ways and attractive green walk links. Highway space will increasingly become congested, as there is limited opportunity to create more road space, so essential vehicles such as buses and emergency services will have to have priority over cars.

Moving from highways to public transport

Fast-emerging cities are likely to be almost entirely reliant on motorized vehicles, with goods being moved by trucks and people heavily dependent upon private cars, motorbikes and bicycles. This has led to extreme congestion in many emerging cities, with highways at gridlock for much of the day. In cities such as Lagos the traffic jams are so long and so intense, even on the major motorways, that they have become market places. Traders set up between slow moving cars and intensive informal economies have sprung up. Though this local economy may be welcomed, in terms of transport this is a disaster; if goods cannot be moved efficiently and people cannot access jobs with reliable journey times then the city cannot flourish.

▲ As traffic congestion is so bad in Lagos, the traffic is mostly at a standstill and informal trading takes place right on the highway

The key for fast-growing cities is to ensure that public transport investment is planned early so that improvements are delivered quickly to replace car-based travel. As emerging cities grow, the demand for highway capacity increases. The problem is that it is relatively easy and cheap to deliver highways, provided land is still available, but the capacity/demand equation tends to fail fairly quickly as new highways attract cars like moths to light; they become congested almost before the tarmac is dry. There is also a limit to how much of the city can be given over to highways, if one is aiming for a city with good urban realm. In Los Angeles 80% of the land surface is highway and 75% of commuters use a car. This level of car reliance has two very negative outcomes: traffic and pollution. Cities that are recognized as being good models of urban design have much lower proportions of land given over to streets and parking than Los Angeles: in New York it is 22%, in London 23% and in Tokyo 24%.[31]

There is also a practical reason for getting people out of cars and on to public transport, or encouraging them to walk or cycle. It is interesting to consider the relative highway space taken up by different modes of transport. A bus passenger takes just 2 m^2 of space, a walking pedestrian requires about 3 m^2 of space, a moving cycle requires 10 m^2 and a car needs 300 m^2. The image below shows the comparative space occupied by 60 people travelling by car, by bus or cycling.

▲ There is a finite amount of road space in any city; with fewer cars there is more space for quality public realm such as wider pavements, benches, street cafes, trees and flowers

In established cities it is actually very difficult to increase highway capacity as land plots are already established and land values are likely to be so high that land purchase becomes prohibitively expensive. The emphasis must therefore be on more efficient use of the existing highway network and giving priority to essential vehicles; that means fewer private cars. This is unlikely to happen without some form of financial squeeze on car use, such as congestion charging or road pricing. This has been shown to work in London, Stockholm and Singapore, where car traffic has been reduced and pollution levels have fallen.

Even if the use of private cars on the roads is reduced, freight operators will have to operate more efficiently; large trucks delivering a single parcel will have to be a

▲ Cities dominated by highway infrastructure are cities for cars not people

thing of the past. Multimodal freight distribution needs to be developed so that goods get close to their final destination before being transferred to delivery vehicles. This will inevitably involve radical controls, incentives and logistics infrastructure, consolidating freight at termini and scaling down local distribution to smaller vehicles.

Parked cars have a negative impact on the streets. Most cars probably spend the majority of their life parked, taking up road space that could be used for cycle lanes and wider pavements for pedestrians and tree planting. In the UK it is estimated that cars spend 96% of their life parked and inevitably deteriorating. It makes far more sense for people living in cities to use a rental or club car, and it is far cheaper than owning a car.

The case for walking and cycling

The question often asked is why all the emphasis on walking and cycling if you have a good public transport network? The case for better walking and cycling environments is partly to do with transport capacity and partly about social issues. Most cities will struggle to maintain sufficient public transport capacity at peak times and removing a relatively small percentage of the demand can make the difference between long queues or getting on the bus. Many public transport journeys are just a few stops on the public transport network, which are distances that can easily be walked or cycled. We have feet at the bottom or our legs and we actually like to use them provided the public realm is pleasant. If transport planners start by thinking about feet first, and then thinking about public transport as being the means for us to use our feet in different places across the city, then people will walk further and above all they will be healthier. Pavements do need to be wide enough to accommodate wheelchair users, people with buggies and luggage and they must also address the needs of those with mobility impairment.

For a city to be vibrant it needs people walking around, talking to and knowing each other. This is a fundamental aspect of citizenship and living in a city. For this to happen spontaneously, the urban realm needs to be attractive, convivial and feel safe. For this reason cities need ensure that the public realm is well designed and well maintained.

Travel demand management

The environmental impact of car travel is gradually being accepted, but in many places, where public transport is not yet sufficiently developed, it will be difficult to persuade people to leave their cars behind and to use alternative forms of transport. A central theme of moving towards more sustainable transport is about behaviour change and getting people to understand the benefits of the alternatives to car travel. Cities have to drive the green agenda and develop transport policies that focus on improving public transport services and an understanding of the importance of sustainable travel.

The German federal government has used strong integrated land use and transport policies to bring about change. From the mid 1970s it did not allow either motorways or high-speed lanes within cities, thus deflecting a high proportion of cars to the periphery of cities. They also used pricing as a tool, having high sales taxes on cars and fuel and policies that favoured clean technology and energy efficiency. Freiburg is an exemplar in delivering sustainable transport; it brought about a significant change by reviewing its land-use policy and public transport provision and over three decades cycle trips tripled, public transport ridership doubled and the share of car journeys fell.[32]

Transport infrastructure and maintenance funding

Transport systems need certainty over their investment programmes. The planning and delivery is long so funding certainty should ideally have a 20–30–year horizon and should be outside political 'short-termism'. A city's transport plan has to assess priorities and ensure that the most effective improvements are embarked upon first. There will often be political pressure to deliver something 'sexy', but if it is not value for money, it is poor investment.

There is much emphasis on developing electric cars and though infinitely more desirable than conventional cars, they are unlikely to have a significant role in future cities as there simply is not enough road space to accommodate more cars. It would be much more useful to develop this technology for delivery vans and service vehicles, which will always have to be part of city transport systems.

High technology

High-speed and hi-tech solutions such as Maglev and bullet trains are likely to play an increasing role in the public transport mix, but they are more likely to form part of the intercity connectivity. These systems are expensive to build and operate, so how the fares are integrated with other options is key. The high-speed Maglev rail link from Shanghai's international airport is being underused as it is priced significantly higher than the parallel metro line. The balance between fare price and convenience needs careful consideration, but there is no point in having highly sophisticated systems if they are not integral to the main transport network.

6

Feeding the City and Taking Care of the Environment

'The future is not something we enter. The future is something we create.'

Leonard I. Sweet

ALL THAT MATTERS

To understand feeding the city, you have to understand how food is produced. Feeding over 9 billion people by 2050 may be difficult, particularly if the developed world carries on thinking that the problem can be resolved by ever more intensive farming. Farming practices will need to change, particularly in terms of their impact on the environment; Rachel Carson's 1962 book *Silent Spring* was a prescient warning about the environmental damage of intensive farming. Agricultural practice is going to have to focus on efficient production, which livestock farming is not, and it is inevitable that people will need to reduce their meat consumption. Intensive farming methods work the land hard and they depend on mechanized processes, pesticides and fertilizers and they do not support biodiversity. Good biodiversity is our insurance for food security. Many believe that intensive farming has now peaked and that smaller and smarter is the future of farming.[33]

The difficulty of changing our relationship to the environment was highlighted eloquently by Professor Gus Speth:

'I used to think that the top global environmental problems were biodiversity loss, eco-system collapse and climate change; I thought with 30 years of good science we could address these

problems, but I was wrong. The top environmental problems are selfishness, greed and apathy – to deal with these, we need a spiritual and cultural transformation and we scientists don't know how to do that.'

Livestock farming requires about 15 times as much land as arable farming. According to the UN Food and Agriculture Organization (FAO), the global livestock sector represents about 40% of global agricultural output. In 2009, 60 billion livestock animals were eaten across the globe.[34] Meat and dairy animals now account for a staggering 20% of all terrestrial animal biomass and use 30% of the earth's entire land surface; a further 33% of all arable land is used for producing livestock feed. The demand for land for livestock is the main driver of deforestation, especially in Latin America where some 70% of former forests in the Amazon have been turned over to grazing.[35] With finite land available, it is clearly going to be difficult to maintain the current levels of meat production. We cannot keep clearing forests to create new farmland, but agronomists believe that if we use more of the existing land for arable farming then the planet's future population can be fed.

Furthermore, livestock production impacts water supplies in two ways, in terms of consumption and in terms of pollution. Livestock production uses vast amounts of water, both directly for drinking and indirectly as part of the production of their feed. Also, the livestock industry is among the most damaging sectors for water resources, with animal waste, antibiotics, hormones and chemicals all contributing to water pollution and overgrazing causing the land to become compacted, thus preventing replenishment of ground water. Livestock feed crop production is also contributing to biodiversity loss; 15 out of 24 important ecosystems are now assessed as in decline, with livestock identified as a culprit.

The 2006 FAO report _Livestock's Long Shadow_ reported that the livestock sector accounts for 18% of CO_2 deriving from human-related activities. However, the environmental scientist Robert Goodland has challenged the 18% figure and claims it is, in fact, 51% when you add in animal respiration, the loss of natural carbon sequestration by the forests that are cut down, the impact of forest burning, livestock feed production and the full impact of refrigeration and transport. Robert Goodland believes that livestock production must be cut by 25% by 2017, the date when the first tipping point of irreversible climate change will be reached (widely agreed by top experts and the IPCC). He says that 'a modest change in diet is possibly the only way to prevent climate change' and suggests an immediate 25% cut in meat production, as a minimum, and ideally moving to a low or meat-free diet. He believes this is achievable now, while the alternatives for cutting greenhouse gas emissions that are being proposed, such as moving to renewable clean energy, will take at least 20 years.[36]

Vandana Shiva, an environmental anti-globalization activist, is also convinced that intensive agriculture is destroying our land. She is an advocate of small-scale organic farming, and believes that the world can feed itself and retain biodiversity by shifting the emphasis away from intensive agriculture to small-scale farms. When questioned on the BBC in 2013 about how we will be able to attract young people into farming since it is not a glamorous profession she was dismissive:

> 'If you treat farming as glamorous, I will go into farming; if you treat speculating with other people's money that may bring down whole countries as glamorous, then I will go into banking. Glamour is assigned to certain tasks by politicians.'

She is convinced that small-scale organic farms are capable of feeding the world and that this form of farming is more profitable and will deliver ecological and food security. She believes that India could, in this way, produce enough good food for two Indias and still maintain biodiversity.[37]

Cities can actually become part of the food revolution and ensure food resilience by growing fruits, vegetables and herbs within their boundaries. Small patches of land, street corners, parks, communal gardens and even containers on balconies and roofs can all produce fruit and vegetables. When the Soviet Union collapsed and Cuba lost its main trading partner in 1989, Havana was plunged into a food shortage. Almost overnight people started planting their own crops in any vacant corner or plot, and it is estimated that up to 90% of Havana's fresh produce now comes from local urban farms and gardens within the city. Sophisticated organic urban farms, 'organopónicos', are run independently by the community entirely on organic principles, and the produce is sold locally, so it comes fresh and with an extremely low carbon footprint. Individuals are growing edible produce everywhere in the city and the gardens are open to the street and part of the local community, attracting young people who appreciate their value.

The urban farming concept is now spreading to cities across the globe. Across the USA they are springing up in cities, kicking back at the food economy dominated by intensive farming and giant supermarkets. Food security is also driving this; most cities only have a week's worth of food. Across Africa urban farms are being set up, partly to provide poverty alleviation through job creation, but also to tackle poor diet head-on by providing plenty of fresh produce right in the heart of the city.

Singapore has taken a more hi-tech approach to urban farming. It has developed a commercial vertical farm to make local fresh produce more available to its millions of citizens. Sky Green Farms currently produces three types of vegetables and although the produce costs a little more than imported it is selling out as local people vote for 'fresh'. The vegetables are grown in 9 m-tall vertical aluminum towers. Singapore has set a target of 10% of vegetables to be grown locally in the near future.

Allotments and community gardens and city farms are springing up on leftover land in many cities. These green oases are bringing together dislocated communities and minority groups and it is also recognized that they have special therapeutic benefits for people suffering anxiety and stress. There is no reason why cities should not produce a significant proportion of their food within the city and it will bring down the carbon footprint of the food, help to reduce the city's heat island effect and will improve air quality. Edible cities are the future!

Life in the City

'Cities have the capability of providing something for everybody, only because, and only when, they are created by everybody.'

Jane Jacobs

ALL THAT MATTERS

The preceding chapters have talked mostly about functionality and making the city run smoothly so that people can move about with ease and their physical needs are taken care of. There is also another aspect to urban life, which is equally important, and which will make the difference between merely existing and having a fulfilling life that feeds the soul and the need for human companionship and creativity. This is the complex mix of leisure, social and cultural facilities that make up a vibrant city, without which it would be a dull place. Ensuring that there is sufficient opportunity for people to socialize, stay healthy and feed their cultural needs is a fundamental aspect of what makes a good city. As homes become smaller, places outside the home will increasingly be an important platform for leisure and social activity. Cultural and entertainment institutions as well as open space will, in future, increasingly become the new 'living rooms' where many people will socialize. There needs to be sufficient local places where people of all ages, social groups and faiths can meet, play, interact and exercise.

London is renowned for its parks and open space; in fact 46% of London's surface is open space. San Francisco has 25% open space but Los Angeles only has 10%;[38] this lack of open space leads to isolation and results in sterile urban realm where no one knows their neighbours or local community. The public realm it is where most of the informal aspects of citizenship happens, it is the stage for social interaction, where we might get to know our neighbours and develop a sense of belonging to our local community. It is all the open space between buildings – town squares, parks, gardens, streets, pavements or street corners – the parts we inhabit when we are not indoors. It is also where we walk when we are travelling between places, where we might jog or go to sit and contemplate.

Cities that do not manage the public realm are usually crime ridden, hostile and unpleasant. It is a well-known fact that if an area has broken windows it is likely to attract anti-social behaviour and the same goes for grubby neglected public spaces. The public realm does have to be looked after and this often comes down to ownership. In new large-scale developments it is common to see the public realm privately owned and managed. A high-quality public realm is known to enhance property values, so developers prefer to retain ownership so that they can ensure the quality of management. However, this has serious implications for public right of access and gathering and the democratic right to be able to congregate in parts of the city. This became a moot point in London during the Occupy protests, where it was clear that when open space was 'private', the protestors could be evicted by the police. In Hong Kong, the thousands of migrant domestic workers congregate in open spaces all over the city on their day off and meet their friends. As their home quarters are generally too small for socializing, the city becomes their living room.

The best cities invest in the public realm both in terms of maintaining it but also in terms of ensuring that the public space is fit for people, accessible and as green as possible, and that it has good street furniture. All the leading large cities that rank highly on the 'livability' index have high quality public realm and open space. There has been a revolution in upgrading and redesign of the public realm in the last couple of decades, as city managers have come to understand that this aspect of the city is as important as fine signature buildings and fabulous transport systems. The public realm will give a place its local identity and very much influence how a local community behaves, and if it is well designed it will be full of people, which is what makes it attractive to us and makes us feel safe. These spaces must be designed for all ages and abilities and must be well lit so that women and vulnerable people do not feel threatened at night.

Open space will always be at a premium, and as cities grow there will be more and more people potentially occupying the same space. It is therefore imperative that the planning system ensures that the supply of open and green space is added to, by including balconies and useable roof spaces. Trees are an essential component of a healthy city. Not only do they produce oxygen for us to breathe; they also help to control CO_2 and other dangerous gases by absorbing and storing them. They also reduce dangerous particulates in the air such as dust, ash, pollen and smoke (which are harmful to our lungs) by filtering them with their leaves, branches and stems. Very importantly they help to control the urban 'heat-island' effect by creating welcome shade and by the cooling effect of evaporation during hot summers.

Managing urban drainage is an important aspect of public realm design. If our cities are nothing but hard surfaces then rainwater cannot be absorbed and will be forced into the drainage system, which will be under pressure to cope and, importantly, little of the rain gets into the ground to replenish underground water courses. By including ample soft landscaping we can ensure that water is absorbed into the ground and contaminated road runoff water can be filtered by plants. Well-considered planting will also support biodiversity and be the stage for us to enjoy the birds and bees.

Staying fit and healthy in the city is a challenge for all. The public realm must include ample local playgrounds for children of all ages, places where adults can walk and jog, and, equally importantly, where elderly people can exercise and move about in comfort and safety.

The public realm is also an important part of the public transport network. It provides the short cuts and nice walks to where we go shopping or pick up public transport and should also provide access for safe cycling.

Heritage, history and memory are also an intrinsic part of the public realm and contribute to the distinctiveness of places, and they help to create a sense of belonging as people can relate to the history of a place. Of course, not all cities are old and new cities will need to develop their own identity and culture; this must be allowed to flourish and grow locally by the local communities.

Culture is what stimulates the creative in us, and a city that supports cultural activities that are available to all social groups will be rich cities. A city should also be able to accommodate the cultural festivals of all its citizens as well as ephemeral art and celebrations and events, fixed or impromptu; all the things that form our life experiences and make it all worthwhile. It is generally recognized that cities or neighbourhoods that have artist communities are exciting and dynamic, but the problem for artists is finding affordable workspaces. As a society we have always, from the dawn of civilization, valued art and how it enriches our lives in many ways, but our modern cities are making it increasingly difficult for young talent to survive. Affordable workspace, just like affordable housing, should be part of what a city offers. This will need new ownership models, so that workplace rents can be controlled for those who need them. It is incumbent upon city governments to consider how to provide this if they want an innovative economy.

Cafes, restaurants, markets and public gathering places are a key part of life in a city; they are what make it vibrant and alive. If city planners do not consider this aspect of city living, life will be dull and unrewarding. These activities support the local economy and will generate new economic growth and opportunity. Hopefully the current obsession with shopping malls, which combine consumerism with social gathering, entertainment and other activities will give way to more flexible cityscapes.

What is for sure is that the majority of us are not going to be living in Ebenezer Howard's Garden Cities as he conceived them, nice cosy houses in green leafy suburbs, but the megacities we are now building can be 'garden cities' if we plan properly and ensure that the public realm is as important as all the infrastructure and built fabric and that we make good use of all our places, including building roofs (though the Chinese idea of building suburbia on the rooftops of buildings is probably taking the suburban dream a bit too far).

▲ Chinese take on the garden suburb – villa on the roof of a shopping mall in Zhuzhou

Many established cities are getting better at re-inventing themselves and making good use of redundant infrastructure. New York has invested in converting an old elevated railway line into a linear park in the sky, the High Line, which is now not just a local place for people to walk and dwell, but has actually become a tourist attraction in its own right. In London, the 2012 Olympics was an opportunity to regenerate an area that had been allowed to decline through neglect and pollution. By burying electricity pylons and cleaning up the contaminated land, London has gained a new park and wetland and a new city quarter has been created. Shanghai has converted an old abattoir into a complex of shops, restaurants and business units. We do not have to tear down everything we no longer use.

Public realm design must be inclusive and truly public so all can feel free to enjoy it and are not excluded through prejudice, 'gating' or screening out people because of their appearance; a decent society will share the freedom of the city with everyone.

The proportion of elderly people in the population is ever growing; at the same time the proportion of younger people (who traditionally took care of the older generation) is falling. Today, about one tenth of world population is over 60 years old and by 2050, this age group will account for one fifth of total world population. This change in demographics will present challenges for governments in terms of social care and pension provision, but the city fabric will also need to adapt to accommodate an increasingly older population. The public realm needs to be accessible to people with walking aids and wheelchairs, traffic lights need to consider a slower walking pace and there should be ample seating, as the elderly have a greater need for periodic rest. Cafes, meeting places, sports and leisure facilities all need to address the needs of the elderly, in terms of access as well as cost. An incredibly important aspect, which is so often overlooked, is the provision of public toilet facilities. Parks and open spaces should have more sheltered areas where the elderly can observe the activity without being threatened by it. The whole community benefits from the participation of older people and the city must be inclusive and must encourage them to be part of the community.

Finally, there is the issue of security. Police forces, local governments and city managers are increasingly overseeing what we do. Surveillance is creeping in everywhere.

Britain is arguably the most spied-upon nation on earth. CCTV, databases, biometrics, 'smart' systems, our credit cards and mobile phones are tracking most of our movements and actions most of the time. The argument is that this is for our own security, that we are under attack from outside forces that are infiltrating our lives. However, as controls and systems are imposed in order for us to access various places, if we do not have the right chip or appearance we will be excluded, and that is most likely to affect the poor, those without the gizmos we need to 'wand' our way through life. It will have a growing impact on those less fortunate, it will constrain lives and the freedom to enjoy the city. How and where this technology is applied should be more open to democratic discussion.

▲ Cities need to feel safe and secure, but the proliferation of surveillance and security measures can generate high levels of tension

8

Sustainable Cities and the Future Possible

'The best way to predict the future is to invent it.'

Theodore Hook

ALL THAT
MATTERS

Sustainability

The term 'sustainability' is much misunderstood. It was originally coined and defined in the UN report *Our Common Future*,[39] also known as the *Brundtland Report*, in 1987. It described sustainable development as the kind of development that meets the needs of the present without compromising the ability of future generations to meet their own needs.

Robert Goodland, an environmental scientist and former longtime adviser to the World Bank, describes sustainability as 'seeking to sustain global life-support systems indefinitely'.[40] He argues that social sustainability depends upon strong civil society and investment in human capital, such as education, health and food, and that economic sustainability ultimately depends on environmental sustainability.

Pessimistic prophecies about the future abound, such as Stephen Emmott's recent book *10 Billion*, in which he suggests that the human species is incapable of changing its ways. However, Professor Danny Dorling, in his book *Population 10 Billion*, published almost at the same time as Emmott's, sees many reasons to be optimistic about our future, such as falling birth rates and the gaining of women's rights.[41] He predicts that the population explosion will end 'peacefully' in about 2050. He is sanguine about our future, provided we change our ways. It is easy to think that the problems are overwhelming, but the positive signs are already here; it is just that the pessimists have the monopoly on being heard.

Hans Rosling, Professor of Global Health at Karolinska Institutet in Sweden, has researched the evolution of health and prosperity. He believes: 'We can stop population growth, we can eradicate poverty, we can solve the energy and the climate issues, but we have to make the right investments ... I know a good world is possible if we leave emotion aside and just work analytically.' Rosling claims to be neither an optimist nor a pessimist, but a 'possibilist'. He calls for those who advocate this position 'practical possibilists'. For Rosling, the important question is not how many of us are alive, but rather how we choose to live. He believes we must invest in social and health-related infrastructure to tackle inequality. Both Dorling and Rosling see war as our greatest threat and agree that peace is most likely to prevail in a world of equality, where all can read and write and have equal access to opportunity.[42]

Ecological footprints

The concept of ecological footprints, a measure of how much land a particular city requires to support itself, can help to understand how a city impacts the global system as a whole and highlight the need to change. Herbert Girardet calculated in 1995 that London required an area equivalent to the entire UK to support it. This was later recalculated in 2000 in a footprint study called *City Limits*,[43] which found that the ecological footprint was, in fact, 293 times its geographical area or roughly twice the size of the UK. For the earth to maintain its equilibrium, cities need to reduce their overall impact, so knowing what this is has to be the starting point.

It is now widely accepted that we need to reduce CO_2 emissions to prevent catastrophic climate change, and many nations have now signed up to targets. Step one is to reach a peak and then start reducing. China has declared that it could reach peak emission by 2026, but at a huge investment cost in its electricity generating industry of $216 billion. It plans to cap all emissions by 2016 and is already trialling 'cap-and-trade' schemes in seven provinces.

Establishing peak emissions is only one step on the journey; the next is to reach carbon neutrality. Four nations are now vying to be the first to become carbon neutral; Iceland, New Zealand, Norway and Costa Rica have signed up to go zero carbon by joining the Climate Neutral Network. Copenhagen has, separately, declared its aim to become the world's first carbon-neutral capital city by 2025. The fact that four nations and a city have publicly committed to this gives hope that it is possible for most cities to become carbon neutral within a reasonable time.

Cap-and-trade is one of the strategies driving carbon reduction. The 'cap' sets a limit on emissions, and this is gradually lowered to reduce the amount of carbon that is released into the atmosphere. The 'trade' works on the principle of creating carbon allowances and a market for trading these; if the allowance is not needed because the reductions have already been achieved then the allowance will be surplus and free to trade, thus creating a financial incentive to speed up the process of conversion.

Tokyo introduced a cap-and-trade approach to reduce pollution and greenhouse gas emissions in 2010. The scheme, which is the first for an urban centre, requires large commercial, industrial and government buildings to cut their carbon emissions by energy efficiency or emissions trading. In its first year, participants cut emissions by 15% (compared to 2000 levels) and by the end of 2012 reductions were at 23% overall. Many participating buildings have now met emissions reduction targets set for 2019, and the program is driving public awareness of climate change.

Sustainable planning

In many emerging cities, responsibility for the city will come under the umbrella of national government and it will not always be easy to have an integrated strategic approach to planning. Cities need to be encouraged to establish strong governance. When power was devolved to the Greater London Authority in 2000, it happened because Londoners had an understanding that its function would be unequivocally strategic. As a result of London having direct control over its investments it has been transformed since 2000.

For a city to grow sustainably it must have a vision that unambiguously sets out how it will adapt and accommodate growth over time. Without this, growth will not necessarily occur in the right places or at the right density, and will potentially obstruct future opportunities for critical infrastructure projects, making their delivery either impossible or very expensive. All the elements of the city need to be considered in a comprehensive and integrated way. Analysis of a city's land uses and open spaces is an essential aspect of understanding what already exists and what is needed and where, to ensure holistic development. Integrated spatial development strategies need to have reasonable timescales of about 20 years, though 30–40 years for infrastructure aspects is useful to make sure that current schemes are compatible with future proposals and to ensure that they interface efficiently. Spatial plans must ensure that housing delivery and public transport are linked; building suburbs or satellite cities that are not connected by public transport should not even be contemplated.

As development and infrastructure proposals come forward it is important to look at all the aspects of their impact; what may solve one problem may cause unforeseen consequences on other aspects of the city. In the UK Integrated Impact Assessment (IIA) tools that take a holistic approach and review a wide range of impacts including environmental, health and social are now being used to review major proposals.

Spatial planning is necessarily a top-down approach to make sure growth happens in an orderly way and that critical infrastructure is delivered in a timely fashion. At the other end of the spectrum is the bottom-up approach that comes from the local communities, which should have the opportunity to contribute to the planning process and have some control over their destiny. The Transition Movement, a process of steering development by the local people, has been taking hold in recent years. Towns and neighbourhoods are declaring themselves to be Transition towns or places where decisions will only be made with the participation of the local communities. It is a kickback to remotely planned regeneration that has tended to parachute in monocultural solutions, driven by preconceptions of financial viability.

Sustainable density and mixed use

The ten densest megacities in the world, Dhaka, Mumbai, Karachi, Manila, Lagos, Kolkata, Delhi, Seoul-Incheon, Mexico City and Tehran, have densities ranging from 25,400 to 115,200 people per square mile.[44] By comparison the density of London is 12,331 people per square mile;[45] the Los Angeles greater urban area is 7,000 people per square mile and the New York greater urban area 5,319 people per square mile.[46]

In his book *Planet of Cities* Shlomo Angel suggests that cities should have densities that are 'not too high and not too low'. That is probably not as non-committal as it sounds, as a city's ability to support density has a direct relationship to its infrastructure. When Angel talks about density being 'not too high and not too low' he is talking about what is appropriate for a particular city, its predicted growth trajectory and its ability to deliver the necessary infrastructure. Cities can be very dense and still pleasurable, provided they have the infrastructure to guarantee a decent life for all their residents, not just the wealthy.

City planners argue that cities must be compact, as this is more efficient. By having dense compact cities of mixed use, the distances people have to travel by public transport are reduced and many of their daily needs can be reached locally on foot or cycle. There will also be economies of scale when delivering public services. There are plenty of arguments for and against the compact city model. The compact city is more likely to preserve the countryside around it, the infrastructure networks are more efficient and communities are more likely to be cohesive. On the other hand compact cities lead to crowding, lack of light and air, over-burdening of infrastructure and unaffordable land for housing. However, there are plenty of established cities with high-density populations that offer a high quality of life. London is a good example: it has a relatively high density, but still has 46% open space and only a low proportion of high-rise housing. Another driver for compact cities has to do with climate change issues; studies have shown that high-density cities lead to lower per capita energy consumption. The indisputable fact is that low-density cities have heavy car use and are unable to sustain adequate public transport, as the services are uneconomical.

Mixed use in planning terms means having most categories of building types within a district; typically residential property, office buildings, commercial shops, leisure and civic buildings. This means there will be a higher proportion of people working, shopping and spending leisure time locally and not travelling for work or shopping. In recent decades, the worst damage to city centres has been caused by ever larger shopping centres being built outside or at the edge of cities. The consequence of this has been dying city centres, as the shops have gone out of business. Cities that have brought activities such as retail, cafes, restaurants and social gathering back to their centres have managed to create vibrant local communities.

Sustainable communities

Rio de Janeiro is well known for its slums, or favelas, and the city has launched a programme, Morar Carioca, to upgrade them by 2020 into recognized city communities. Roughly one fifth of the city's residents, around 232,000 households, live mostly without basic sanitation and with little in the way of building standards. Under the plan, clean water and waste collection will be introduced and residential buildings will be improved. The programme will bring obvious social, health and safety benefits, will cut emissions, water pollution, and soil erosion, but crucially the favelas will be 're-urbanized'. Importantly, this programme will not displace the favela dwellers, but will maintain their communities intact and the citizens will be integrated into the mainstream of the city.

It is widely agreed that equality is one of the fundamental building blocks of sustainable communities. This does not mean that everyone will be equally rich; rather it means that all will be able to read and write and have equal opportunities in life. There will always be the richer and the poorer, but hopefully the gulf will narrow. The key is 'opportunity' and reducing the sense of separation. Good design should address this and make places feel accessible to all. Indian architect Rahul Mehrotra sees breaking down the barriers between the wealthy professional classes and the working classes as fundamental to the process of breaking down the social barriers that exist in India, and he has developed a concept of 'soft thresholds' in his building designs. He designs them so that they are literally or metaphorically transparent, so that the separation between rich and poor is broken down and the poor can penetrate the world of the rich. Buildings like this can act as powerful symbols of equality and opportunity.

Sustainable design, culture and heritage

There is no such thing as the perfect plan, masterplan or ideal city. Each solution has to be a response to its context and physical environment. However, there are some key principles that apply to all cities. The layout and street pattern should have a logic to it so that you understand how the city fits together. Permeability is very important, so you can walk through all neighbourhoods; vast privatized city blocks and gated communities have no place in an equitable city. The balance of built fabric and open space is critical to making the city liveable. An important aspect of city design is distinctiveness and local character. It is difficult to feel part of a city if everywhere looks the same and is bland and ordinary. Cities are great when they offer richness and diversity, the unexpected and the predicable, the beautiful and the gritty.

Enrique Peñalosa, former mayor of Bogotá, has been hailed as one of the great city mayors of recent times.

He promoted a city model giving priority to children and public spaces and restricting private car use, building hundreds of kilometres of pavements, bicycle paths, pedestrian streets, greenways and parks. He led efforts to improve Bogotá's marginal neighbourhoods through citizen involvement; planted more than 100,000 trees; created a new, highly successful bus-based transit system; and turned a deteriorated downtown avenue into a dynamic pedestrian public space. Above all, through his 'From living hell to living well' campaign he helped transform the city's attitude from one of negative hopelessness to one of pride and optimism. His view is that 'A city can be friendly to people or it can be friendly to cars, but it can't be both'; for him the city is the 'public living room'.

Sustainable Energy

The source of our future energy will have a direct impact on the environment, pollution and climate change. Alternatives to fossil fuels have to be developed. For countries such as the UK, energy from alternatives such as wind and wave power are obvious; mountainous areas are likely to expand hydroelectric production (though they will face opposition if this involves damming) and desert climates can obviously exploit solar energy. There is also the potential to extract energy from waste and sewage and to exploit geothermal energy.

Much of our infrastructure relies on electricity, but as was discussed in Chapter 3, high-voltage electrical transmission grids are very inefficient. However, it is possible to generate electricity locally and in a sustainable way; decentralized energy brings power generation and distribution right down to the local level. Decentralized energy is generally described as the wide range of technologies that do not rely on the high-voltage electricity transmission network or the gas grid. Decentralized energy plants are generally small-scale plants that supply electricity and they can operate at any scale, from the micro level of a single appliance through to major districts or even whole cities, and they may well sell surplus electricity back into another distribution network. By linking decentralized energy systems with other local systems, such as heat from waste, then further efficiencies can be gained.

The generation systems within a decentralized system can include micro-generation such as solar panels, wind turbines, biomass or waste burners, combined heat and power (CHP) plants, geothermal energy and heat pumps. CHP plants, even when the fuel is not from a renewable source, are much greener than conventional energy generation. Local generation reduces transmission losses, lowers carbon emissions, and increases security of both supply and prices. Decentralized energy can easily be incorporated into new development as well as into existing communities. London is aiming for a quarter of its energy to be from decentralized sources by 2025, and although it is recognized that changing to decentralized energy will initially require an investment of £5–7 billion, it will achieve a tenfold CO_2 reduction. The concept of decentralized energy generation is gradually becoming mainstream in many European and worldwide cities.

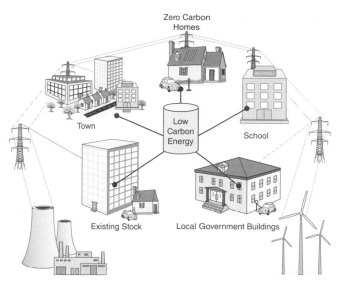

▲ Diagram of a local decentralized energy system

Conventional electricity generation produces vast amounts of heat as a by-product, as do most of our machines, and we throw it away. We can capture and use it. The concept of heat networks is now being developed in cities. Power plants are major heat sources, but heat can also be captured at the smaller scales, such as decentralized energy plants or our transport infrastructure. For example, London Underground produces a lot of heat that is normally removed via vent shafts. There is now a scheme to capture the heat and use it to heat homes in London. In Helsinki, 90% of homes are heated by district heating networks. Though this type of infrastructure is probably out of reach of many emerging cities in the short term, it should be considered as they migrate to greener energy policies.

Cooling is also an issue and accounts for a considerable amount of our energy use. Cooling huge corporate data servers requires significant high-energy air-conditioning. However, data servers can be located remotely and Norway has created a facility, the Green Mountain Data Centre, to cool servers, which they claim will be a zero carbon facility. The servers will be stored in mountain caves and chilled using piped water from the nearby fjord, which is at a constant 8°C. Copenhagen is similarly using cool seawater to cool its office buildings.

Both the heating and cooling systems mentioned above work with what is around us, in nature or produced by our activities, instead of using energy. By thinking laterally we can probably find zero-carbon solutions for many of our daily operations; innovators have to be encouraged to look for these solutions so cities can reduce their energy consumption and carbon emissions.

Sustainable waste management

Waste collection accounts for huge CO_2 emissions as trucks trundle up and down every street in the city to pick up rubbish. Underground vacuum collection, a system that was pioneered in Sweden in the 1970s, is now slowly being adopted in new developments. The system is based on a number of waste chutes, either within buildings or outside, and a network of underground pipes. The building occupants sort waste into recyclable, organic and non-recyclable packages, before dropping the waste into the appropriate chute. The waste is automatically transported through a fully enclosed system of underground vacuum pipes to a central collection station where it is compacted and stored for collection. The waste trucks then make one single journey to pick up the waste containers when they are full. This system reduces refuse truck miles by up to 90%, thus reducing CO_2 emissions and also relieving highway capacity.

▲ Diagram of the Envac underground vacuum waste extraction system (courtesy of Envac)

Sustainable water

To use water sustainably, we need to understand properly how much we use and waste. It is not just what we use to drink or for bathing; by far the greatest use of water worldwide is for agriculture. So when we consume our food or buy our clothes we are indirectly also consuming considerable amounts of water. A kilogram of beef equates to 15,400 litres of water and 1 kg of cotton will use 10,000 litres of water.[47] This water is generally referred to as virtual or embodied water and can be calculated, but rarely is. When we buy a printed cotton shirt, we are mostly oblivious of the vast quantities of water that will have been used in its production. Thinking about water this way has been developed by the Water

Footprint Network into the concept of 'water footprints', which calculate the total volume of fresh water that is consumed by a community, the environmental impacts of water extraction and delivery, the virtual water in goods and services, and it will also evaluate the pressures being placed on ecosystems. The water footprint can inform decisions about the sustainable and equitable allocation of water, and can raise understanding of the issues if difficult changes to consumption have to be introduced.

Sustainable management of urban rainwater runoff is important in terms of relieving draining systems that are under stress and also, importantly, in ensuring that rainwater finds its way to replenish ground sources. A system know as Sustainable Urban Drainage Systems (SUDS) has been developed to capture and treat surface runoff rainwater naturally, using plant filtration beds incorporated into the road construction, which reduces the amount of storm water that enters drainage systems. Not only does SUDS preserve water, it reduces the cost of urban drainage. This type of water management is gradually being introduced into cities (as well as rural highways) and will in the long term significantly reduce drainage costs and preserve water.

Sustainable sanitation

Human waste is a potential source of energy. Liquid and solid waste needs to be separated, so researchers at the Singapore Nanyang Technological University have developed a new toilet that does just that; it has been dubbed the 'No-mix loo'. Solid waste can be mixed with food waste to produce biogas, and biodiesel can be obtained from urine. Processing human waste is an expensive business so turning it into an energy source makes sense.

Solid human waste can also be processed to extract high-quality phosphorous fertilizer. A new plant at Slough treatment works in the UK is Europe's first 'nutrient recovery reactor'. It turns human waste sludge into bright white odourless phosphorus-rich pellets, which can be used for food cultivation. Phosphorous is an important fertilizer, but a finite resource, and some experts believe that mineable reserves will run out or become very scarce by 2035. Human waste or 'night soil' used to be spread on fields in the past, but because it contains dangerous pathogens and contaminants, its use has now been banned. This is a way to return phosphorous to the food cycle.[48]

Sustainable transport

Megacities will have to invest in green transport infrastructure to bring about more sustainable practice. High-income cities, where car use is high, need a paradigm shift towards green travel and public transport, whereas low-income cities will need to be deflected away from adopting the fossil fuel-reliant infrastructure norms of wealthy nations. Fast metro and light rail schemes are the ultimate aspiration of modern cities, but they take a long time to deliver and are expensive. Public transport does need heavy capital investment as well as revenue subsidy and there is not a city in the world where public transport pays for itself; public transport budgets will always be a significant proportion of a city's expenditure. The emphasis must be on a phased delivery of a variety of public transport options, especially when cities are starting from a low base, with quicker solutions such as bus rapid transit (BRT) system being delivered early, while the more complex metro and rail systems are being built out. The temptation to build ever-bigger highways to alleviate congestion must be resisted.

Underground and rail transport projects have long delivery times and high costs, but there are innovative and cheaper solutions that can be delivered quickly. Bus travel may not have the same appeal as modern metro systems, but the Colombian city of Curitiba was choked with traffic in the 1970s so it introduced a BRT system, high-frequency buses in segregated lanes that performed similarly to an underground system. This low-cost transport solution dramatically changed travel patterns and now 70% of commuters travel by bus. Similarly, in London when in 2000 it set about modernizing its transport system, bus travel was very unpopular because it was unreliable and the infrastructure was degraded. This was not helped by Margaret Thatcher saying 'any man who finds himself on a bus at 26 can count himself a failure'.[49] As a result of modernizing the bus service by introducing bus priority lanes so that buses could get through traffic, real-time information about when a bus would be coming or the location of the next stop, and introducing modern buses, bus passenger miles rose by

60% between 2001 and 2009. Public transport schemes can range from the de luxe integrated systems of cities such as London, Shanghai, Hong Kong and Seoul to the innovative solution of cable cars in Medellin.

Seoul has been rapidly modernizing and is now an exemplar of dense urban planning. Sustainable travel and urban realm quality have been at the forefront of its investment in the city and as a result it is highly accessible and travel is very cheap compared to other world cities. The city has the most track distance of any underground system in the world, serving over 7 million people every day, which is highly integrated with an extensive network of clean buses, as well as water taxis, walking and cycling. One of the citiy's boldest moves was to remove an elevated highway that ran directly over the 3.5-mile course of Cheonggyecheon Stream, transforming the river course into an urban park.

▲ Seoul took the bold step of removing an elevated highway and restoring a buried river in a new urban park

The city of Medellin in Colombia has employed an innovative solution to solve the acute lack of transport for the inhabitants of the slums on the hillsides that surround the city. There was no public transport and the road network was poor, so getting to work in the city centre was a laborious ordeal often taking up to two hours. The city came up with an ingenious solution of introducing a cable-car system that would link the barrios to the city centre; a solution that was relatively easy to install as only a few pylons had to be inserted into the dense city fabric, and was also relatively inexpensive (compared to upgrading the roads for buses or a rail option). It has transformed life in the barrios and has also had wide-reaching regeneration impacts. Delivering urgent infrastructure does sometime need innovative thinking.

▲ Bringing public transport to the informal settlements on the hills surrounding Medelin, Colombia, was a challenge simply solved by installing a cable-car system – it has transformed how people get to work

Most cities will need strategies to reduce car use and this may be difficult if public transport infrastructure is inadequate. Charging for using cars is an effective tool to reduce car use and this can be done in a number of ways, such as putting heavy taxes on cars and fuel, or charging cars to enter certain areas, or charging for road miles used. In 2000 average traffic speeds in central London were probably slower than in the Victorian era, at about 5 miles per hour. The London congestion charge scheme aimed to reduce congestion in the central area by charging for entry or passing through. It had an instant impact and in the first 12 months reduced traffic by 21% and congestion by 30%. It also had the added benefit of increasing cycling by 43% and reducing accidents and air pollution. Singapore has the Electronic Road Pricing system, which has resulted in some of the lowest traffic congestion of any major city. Road pricing is likely to become commonplace in the future, not just to reduce traffic in cities, but to reduce the overall number of cars on the highways which connect cities to each other.

Travel demand management is an important aspect of sustainable transport planning. It is usually a combination of strategies to change travel behaviour and provide infrastructure that will make sustainable travel more attractive than car travel. The most effective way to bring about a change in behaviour is to help people understand why change is necessary and how change will make a difference. Ensuring that a greater percentage of journeys are made by walking or cycling is a key part of sustainable transport strategies, but the environment must be conducive; pavements need to be appealing to pedestrians and streets need to cater for cyclists. Metro system maps are for many people their mental-map of the city. The trouble is they do not know the bits in between the stops, so do not know how the city fits together. To overcome this, Transport for London introduced 'Legible London', a system of information signs and maps to assist people to navigate central London. As a result, more people are now walking further and more often, and, above all, are enjoying it.

The growth of digital services and big data holds the potential to revolutionize travel and transport systems for both goods and people in the future. The consequences of the data revolution on transport are likely to be wide ranging. There will probably be increased travel and freight volumes (resulting in part from online shopping), but there is also the potential for safer, faster transport networks with increased capacity and better value and service quality for customers. Vehicles and trains could have high-precision autonomous vehicle controls such as antilock braking systems, which will allow 'virtual coupling', so that they will be able to travel at high speed very close together. It should transform the freight and logistics industry, allowing for optimum routing and network efficiency. These systems are likely to emerge over the next couple of decades and are likely to be an integral part of transport in megacities.

Sustainable housing

Providing affordable housing and tackling the living conditions of the urban poor is always going to be difficult. Differing approaches around the world have been emerging. UN Habitat believes that slum upgrading, rather than slum clearance, is the best approach. What is clear is that if populations are to be resettled, then everything must be done to preserve the community ties that exist. The mechanisms for delivering improvements vary widely, from state-controlled and funded projects to private developer initiatives that combine slum upgrade with development opportunity, or initiatives run by NGOs, charities and international development agencies. In some models, the new housing is owned by the occupants; in others it is rented.

Greater Mumbai is a megacity of about 19 million people, 60% of whom live in very dense informal settlements. One of these, Dharavi, has 600,000 inhabitants and is many contiguous slums built on swamp land; it is the largest slum in the world and the densest with 2.6 million people per square mile. Facilities and sanitation are sparse, there are filthy public toilets and the area is prone to monsoon flooding. Many agencies have been working to improve the lives of the slum dwellers in Mumbai; the government, many NGOs including the National Slum Dwellers Federation (NSDF), the Society for the Promotion of Area Resource Centres (SPARC), which supports the Mahila Milan (decentralized women's collective micro funding), developers, architecture students and above all the dwellers themselves. The concern in Dharavi is that this area is a development opportunity as the land is valuable and the government is asking developers to bid how much of their profit they will give the government, based on them being allowed to build 1.33 m^2 private development for every

1 m² of 'improved' slum development. The city's Slum Rehabilitation Authority stipulates that the new housing units for the poor have to be 21 m² (in the EU the average housing unit size is 76 m²).[50] It is highly questionable whether this formula will deliver adequate improvement in living conditions.

Mankhurd district in Mumbai is a new community, housing 18,500 families who have been moved, mainly from shacks along the railway tracks. Though the units are only 21 m² they have running water, plumbing and their own toilets, privacy and security; above all, the families are given legal title to the property. The children all go to school by school bus and the Mahila Milan has been helping many of the women to become breadwinners in the small-scale local economy and hence more independent. TVs and refrigerators are becoming the norm and rising self-esteem and motivation has improved jobs opportunities. The NSDF, whose members are mainly volunteers from the poor communities, says that housing the poor works best, costs less and is better for the environment when the poor themselves have a say in what is built.

Brazil's social housing initiative to provide social or low-income housing is a programme called 'Minha Casa Minha Vida' or 'My House My Life', which aims to build 2 million low-cost housing units across the country. It is a subsidized loan scheme to get people to build their own. The programme is available to low-income families who normally would not be able to own a home due to lack of income, personal savings or acceptable credit history; it offers as much as 100% financing through the Caixa National Bank at very low interest rates. However, there are problems resulting from hasty construction and many units are small, only 42 m^2, and far from commercial centres and without transport links; it is inevitable that clear parameters must be set for any such scheme.

Istanbul, one of the most rapidly growing cities in the world, has an acute need for affordable housing and it has an added urgency as the city is anticipating future earthquake damage, following the one in 1999 which killed an estimated 35,000 inhabitants. Consequently the government has decided to remove and rebuild 1 million dwellings to make them earthquake proof within 20 years. The government-owned housing agency TOKI builds affordable housing, mainly tower blocks outside the city centre, and a government agency provides low-interest mortgages. Due to the government's determination to deliver earthquake-proof housing, many squatter settlements, or *gecekondular* as they are called in Turkish, are being forcefully evicted, breaking up communities and dislocating the residents from their work; as a result many find they are unable to maintain the mortgage payments they have acquired.

In sub-Saharan Africa 71.8% of urban dwellers live in slums, the highest proportion of slum dwellers in the world.[51] In Kenya the focus is on a new approach, slum upgrading through participation. This involves regularizing tenure security, providing infrastructure improvements, and the construction of communal facilities. This approach ensures that local communities are not treated as 'subjects' of development projects, but rather that they are active participants in the process. Above all this acknowledges the importance of their needs, local knowledge and opinions. The Building in Partnership: Participatory Urban Planning Project in 2001-2004 for the city of Kitale involved surveying the community in order to understand properly the issues so that at the implementation stage their main needs were addressed. Key issues were lack of employment and lack of skills, so the implementation approach was to employ the residents in the construction activity and train them; having the community so closely involved increased both the standard of the work and improved their self-reliance. As the focus is on human capital rather than on expensive building materials, this approach is relatively low cost and has the positive outcome of a population with new skills.

The Brazilian and the Turkish models are based on buying the housing, as opposed to rental; this does mean that the most vulnerable in society are unlikely to benefit. Alternative models are for governments and local authorities to build social housing for affordable rent, which does presuppose that they have access to affordable land and finance. Other models include social landlords who develop intermediate and social rented housing.

Ultimately what is important is the quality of the housing, whether it supports the local community's way of life and whether it guarantees security (regardless of the ownership model). The condition of the urban poor can be drastically improved with the right assistance and the participation of the community. Though UN Habitat is predicting a growth in slum-dwelling populations, there is no reason why this cannot be tackled sensitively and, provided the poor are also helped to gain skills and achieve work, then they will in many cases set about improving their situation themselves.

Sustainable use of buildings

Most of our non-residential buildings are empty and unused for a large proportion of their lives. Schools are mostly empty during the holidays, the weekends and at night. Assuming an average school is open for business 39 weeks of the year, then allowing for 5 out of 7 days' occupation and 10 hours' closure at night, the buildings will only be occupied for 30% of the year. Office and commercial buildings, though not as bad, are probably only occupied 50% of the time. Civic buildings such as libraries, entertainment theatres, sports centres and the like are probably only at best occupied for 50% of their life. We need to re-think the concept of single-use buildings in the future, and develop buildings that serve more than one function, rather than being left empty for long periods. It is an incredible waste of built assets to have them standing empty, and in countries where they are heated, they stand cooling off overnight, giving off the valuable energy that has been pumped into them.

In the developed world building lifespans have been getting shorter and shorter; it is not uncommon for office blocks to be condemned for demolition after 20 years. This is a senseless waste of all the resources embodied in the fabric of the building. We should be innovative about adapting buildings for re-use as well as thinking about 'meanwhile uses' or 'transition uses' for buildings that may have to be redeveloped in the future.

Sustainable ownership

In cities most privately owned cars probably only get used a few hours each weekend at the most, probably less than 2% of the time. So for 98% of the time the car is parked and depreciating in value. It should be our priority to make sure that the use of highly engineered machines with much embodied energy is maximized for their life. This is only likely to happen if we move away from personal ownership of things we do not use regularly. Owning our own car in a city makes little sense but car-sharing schemes and car-club schemes will ensure that the cars are used for the majority of their life. The city of Portland in USA claims to have the world's most successful car-share scheme, Car2go, which has cars all over the city, available 24 hours a day, seven days a week, that can be picked up in one location and dropped off in another part of the city; users are charged for the time they use. Internet sites now facilitate car sharing; in mainland Europe it is not unusual for someone driving from one city to another to take a few passengers who each pay for the ride.

Sustainable relationship with the environment

Biophilia is a term coined by Harvard biologist and conservationist E. O. Wilson to describe how humans are hard-wired to need connection with nature. The need for biophilic places in buildings has been recognized for some time, particularly for their therapeutic qualities in hospitals. However, it is only beginning to be applied to cities as a whole. The concept of a biophilic city is being developed by Professor Tim Beatley at the University of Virginia. He describes biophilic cities as having abundant nature and biodiversity, where the residents can have close contact with nature, and where there is opportunity for outdoor activity. These principles are steadily emerging as it is more widely recognized that urban dwellers have a need for contact with nature and that they enjoy being part of the natural cycle of nature. Cities should offer ample opportunity for people to observe, enjoy and take part in the natural world; it is particularly important for children to experience natural life and gain an understanding of where food comes from.

In 1963, Prime Minister Lee Kuan decided that Singapore needed greening and ordered trees to be planted in the city to enhance the quality of life and to make it distinctive and attractive. As a result the city is now referred to as the garden city with even the highways overhung by mature trees. Biophilia was probably not on his radar, but he had an instinct that cities with trees are pleasant and that they contribute to life quality.

Conclusion

Sir Karl Popper, philosopher and critical rationalist, has been quoted in many sources, but I will quote him again as his positive vision is a good starting point when speculating about future growth and whether we are doomed or have the potential for a bright future in megacities: 'it is our duty not to prophesy evil but rather to fight for a better world'.[52]

I started writing this book feeling that our progress over the next 20 to 30 years will be a hugely difficult challenge, but I am now convinced that we can do this 'project' collectively. There are so many small but exemplary initiatives and so many inspiring advocates for new ways of doing things; we need to listen closely and learn from them. We also need to learn to listen more to local people and their communities. More and more of the inspiring examples of sustainable or best practice that I have come across have emerged from local people.

Future cities will be different, but if we get it right, they will be delightful democratic places where social interaction thrives and people have equal opportunity to lead fulfilling lives. How will they look? They should not be concrete jungles, but rather an amalgam of distinctive neighbourhoods that have abundant green open space, green trees and fresh running water. They can be edible cities, where much of the planting is food, where biodiversity abounds and the inhabitants can get dirt under their fingernails and enjoy the excitement of seeing nature grow. They should be caring cities, where the less privileged, less educated or less 'perfect' are equally valued, where people are happy with less and where your status is not measured by what you have but by how you live. They should be well-managed cities, with good infrastructure and governance systems that function. They should be places where people use less, generate less waste and travel less. They should be cities not driven by economic obsession, but rather by creative obsession.

Ten prehistoric cities, some surviving today

1. **Jericho,** on the West Bank of the river Jordan, is possibly the world's oldest continuously inhabited city. It dates back 11,000 years and has evidence of 20 successive settlements. The Israelites, who were led out of Egypt by Moses, settled there.

2. **Çatalhöyük in southern Anatolia,** Turkey, flourished from about 7500 to 5700 BCE. It is the best preserved Neolithic city and a World Heritage Site. It may have housed up to 10,000 people. It had no streets and access was across the rooftops, with ladders to the houses below.

3. **Evidence suggests that Istanbul,** which has also been known as Byzantium and Constantinople, was inhabited 8,000 years ago. It has served as capital of four empires: the Roman empire, the Byzantine empire, the Latin empire and the Ottoman empire. It is a unique World Heritage Site spanning two continents, linking Europe to Asia across the Bosphorous.

4. **The Mesopotamian walled city of Uruk,** east of the river Euphrates in southern Iraq, was probably one of the largest cities in the world at its height at about 5500–4000 BCE. It is thought to have had a population of 50–80,000.

5. **Thebes (modern Luxor)** was first inhabited about 3200 BCE, and became the capital of the Egypt from the Middle Kingdom. At its height in 2000 BCE it probably

had a population of 80,000. Thebes is best known for its mortuary on the western banks of the Nile, the Valley of the Kings, where the pharaohs were interred in magnificent splendour.

6. **Babylon** is probably best known for the 'Hanging Gardens', which were one of the Seven Wonders of the Ancient World. It was probably founded about 2000 BCE. The gardens were never found and many thought they were simply mythical. However, archaeologist Dr Stephanie Dalley has uncovered evidence that leads her to believe that they were, in fact, built in Nineveh, known at the time as New Babylon.

7. **Athens** is about 3,400 years old. Culture, learning and politics flourished in the fifth and fourth centuries BCE, it was the home of Plato and Aristotle, and has come to be known as the birthplace of democracy. The Acropolis and its various buildings are an early example of sophisticated urbanism and architecturally controlled space.

8. **Myth has it** that Rome was founded in 753 BCE by twins Romulus and Remus (who survived abandonment by being suckled by a she-wolf). The 'Eternal City' of ancient Roman poets, it is one of the most referenced examples of 'perfect' urban realm.

9. **Beijing** is about 3,000 years old and has been the political centre for the last eight centuries. It is famous for its lavish palaces, temples, tombs, gardens, walls and gates. It is a city designed and evolved on a super-scale.

10. **The Inca city of Machu Picchu,** a World Heritage Site, has the aura of being ancient but was probably built in the fourteenth century and housed about 500,000 people.

Ten sources and facts about ecology, environment and sustainability

11. **Raising livestock is an inefficient use of land,** compared to arable farming. Beef rearing needs about 21 m² of land to produce 1 kg of meat, whereas 1.4 m² will yield 1 kg of cereal and 0.3 m² will yield 1 kg of vegetables. In the USA more than 70% of grain and cereal production is fed to farmed animals.

12. **In future the majority of the human population** will live in cities and they will have to be fed. *Silent Spring* by Rachel Carson, published in 1962, was a scientific critique of intensive farming practice. Many of the chemicals she attacked are now banned, but at the time she was pilloried and accused of being a hysterical woman.

13. *The Granite Garden* by Anne Whiston Spirn (1984) is a powerful message that the environment of our cities is a cornerstone to our well-being.

14. *The World Without Us* by Alan Weisman (2007) is a thought-provoking speculation about what would become of our built environment if we were mysteriously to disappear.

15. **Cows produce vast amounts of methane,** which after CO_2 is an important greenhouse gas. Though methane does occur naturally, a significant proportion of current volumes are attributed to cow farts (though fossil fuel production and landfill are also responsible).

16. **City allotments** were probably started in the cities of Philadelphia and New York in the 1800s. Allotments were legalized in London during the First World War, but the 1.5 million at their height across UK have now dwindled to a quarter of a million.

17. *The Making of the Queen Elizabeth Olympic Park* (2012) by **John Hopkins** and **Peter Neal** sets out the concept of sustainable landscaping and how this was implemented in the London Olympic Park.

18. **Hong Kong** is the highest per capita producer of waste. In 2009, 7 million Hong Kong inhabitants generated 6.45 million tons of waste, which equates to 921 kg of solid waste per person.

19. *Sweet and Salt* by **Tracy Metz and Maartje van den Heuvel** sets out how the Netherlands has coped with the constant threat of the sea and how it is preparing for the future.

20. *Green Cities of Europe: Global Lessons in Green Urbanism* (2012) is edited by **Tim Beatley** with various contributors including **Camilla Ween**. This book sets out contemporary sustainable city practice in seven European cities.

Twelve inspirational, seminal and conceptual sources on urbanism

21. *Design of Cities* by **Edmund Bacon** (1967) remains one of best texts to understand the evolution of urban space concepts from analysis of historic to contemporary cities.

22. *Garden Cities of Tomorrow* by **Ebenezer Howard** (1902) gave rise to the Garden City Movement, the basis for Letchworth and Welwyn. The concept was an early proposal for containing sprawl.

23. *La Ville Radieuse* by architect **Le Corbusier** (1933) was his view of the ideal future city.

24. *London the Unique City* by Steen Eiler Rasmussen (1934) is still one of the best books for understanding London as a complex web of independent forces and Englishness.

25. *Urban Design Since 1945 – A Global Perspective* by David Graham Shane (2011) charts the evolution of post-war large cities.

26. *The Death and Life of Great American Cities* by Jane Jacobs (1961) is a seminal text for most urbanists, which cites modern planning for destroying communities.

27. *The Power Broker: Robert Moses and the Fall of New York* by Robert A. Caro (1974) is a biography of the man who shaped the evolution of New York City for much of the twentieth century.

28. *Cities of Tomorrow* by Professor Peter Hall (new edition 2002) is a significant text on planning history and practice in the twentieth century.

29. In *Planet of Cities* (2012), Shlomo Angel challenges the 'Containment Paradigm' and proposes a new 'Making Room Paradigm'.

30. In *The Global City: New York, London, Tokyo* (2001), Saskia Sassen charts the influence of these cities on global economics and globalisation.

31. *Maximum City: Bombay Lost and Found* by Suketu Mehta (2012) is a powerful personal view of Bombay's challenges today.

32. Architect Giambattista Nolli's 1748 plan of Rome became an important influence on architects and urban planners for its graphic technique of distinguishing built and public space, and representing enclosed public spaces as open civic space.

Six extreme challenges: divided and joined-up cities

33. **Jerusalem's** 6,000-year history has been one of continued strife. It has been destroyed twice, besieged 23 times, attacked 52 times, captured and recaptured 44 times. Today East Jerusalem is under Israeli control. It was annexed by Israel following the Six Day War but this is not recognized as being legal by the International Community, which refers to this area as 'Palestinian territory occupied by Israel'.

34. **Following the Second World War,** Berlin was divided into four sectors under the control of the United States, Britain, France and the Soviet Union. The Berlin Wall was built in 1961 to separate East Germany under Soviet control from the West. The wall was a powerful symbol of division and was eventually torn down in 1989, signalling the end of the Cold War.

35. **During the Lebanese civil war from 1975 to 1990,** Beirut was a divided city between the Muslim west and the Christian east. Since the end of the war the city has been attempting to re-build community bridges, though tensions still remain.

36. **Nicosia is Europe's last remaining and longest divided city.** Since 1974 the Turkish and Greek Cypriot sectors have been separated by a UN-patrolled no-man's-land.

37. **Malmø and Copenhagen saw strength and economic advantage in unity and better connections,** so they built the 5-mile Øresund Bridge linking Denmark and Sweden.

38. In *A Tale of Two Cities* by Charles Dickens (1859), London and Paris are woven together in a tale of history and fiction.

Eight extreme locations, records and anomalies

39. **Most northern city:** Longyearbyen, Norway, 78° 13′ N.

40. **Most southerly city (three vie for the title):**

- **Punta Arenas,** Chile, 53° 10′ S
- **Ushuaia,** Argentina, 54° 48′ S
- **Puerto Williams,** Chile, 54° 56′ S.

41. **Equatorial cities:**

- **Singapore,** 1° 17′ N
- **Kuala Lumpur,** Malaysia, 3° 8′ N
- **Bogatá,** Colombia, 4° 35′ N
- **Fortaleza,** Brazil, 3° 46′ S.

42. **The highest city:** La Rinconada, Peru, 5,099 m above sea level.

43. **Some cities below sea level:**

- **Jericho,** West Bank, 258 m below sea level
- **Amsterdam Schiphol airport,** Netherlands, 4 m below sea level
- **New Orleans,** USA, 2 m below sea level.

44. **Wealthiest cities:**

- **Shanghai,** China
- **Moscow,** Russia
- **Chicago,** USA.

45. **Poorest city:** Potosi, Bolivia.

46. **Most colleges and universities:** probably New York City with over 80.

Eight natural and anthropogenic events that have, and probably will in the future, shape cities

47. **Pompeii was buried under the ash of the Mount Vesuvius eruption in 70 CE,** killing an estimated 16,000 people. The last significant eruption was in 1994; greater Naples, with a population of 4 million, lies at its base today.

48. **The Great Fire of London in 1666** destroyed 13,200 houses and 87 churches. Officially only six people died, but it is thought that the poor were not accounted for.

49. **The Great Lisbon earthquake of 1755** killed an estimated 10,000–100,000 and is thought to have been the most deadly earthquake in history.

50. **The eruption of Krakatoa in 1883** is probably the most powerful in modern times; it wiped out 163 villages and killed 36,380 people.

51. **The 1906 San Francisco earthquake** destroyed 80% of the city and killed about 3,000 people.

52. **Istanbul (then known as Constantinople) was hit by a major earthquake in 1509** that killed an estimated 10,000 people. In 1999 the city was again struck by a major earthquake; unofficial estimates put the death toll between 30,000 and 40,000.

53. **Hurricane Katrina in 2005** brought devastation to New Orleans, with 175 mph winds and a storm surge of 6 m,

which left 80% of the city under water. It killed 1,836 and affected an estimated 15 million people.

54. **The 2011 earthquake in Christchurch,** New Zealand, devastated the downtown commercial district, killing 185 people.

Three population and global health sources

55. In *Population 10 Billion* (2013) Danny Dorling charts global population and sets out a positive vision for the future.

56. *Shadow Cities* by Robert Neuwirth (2005) is an extraordinary insight into the life of the urban poor. It is moving, warm, funny, and is one of the most inspiring books you can read about the world's urban poor. See him on YouTube: http://www.ted.com/talks/robert_neuwirth_on_our_shadow_cities.html

57. **Hans Rosling** is professor of Global Health at Karolinska Institutet in Sweden. He is one of the most inspiring believers in the convergence of health and prosperity. Watch his TED talks on YouTube: http://www.ted.com/talks/hans_rosling_shows_the_best_stats_you_ve_ever_seen.html

Ten critical and inspirational thinkers

58. *Small is Beautiful by* E. F. Schumacher (1975) is a remarkable book. He looks at the economics of the West and suggests that our pursuit of profit has led to dysfunctional organizations and inhumane working practices.

59. *Enough* by John Naish (2009) is a critique of our Western obsession with wanting more and more, but he believes we can overcome our urges if we adopt a philosophy of 'enoughism'.

60. *Requiem for a Species* (2010) by Clive Hamilton is an urgent plea for us to get to grips with dealing with climate change. Read the book and watch Clive Hamilton on YouTube: http://www.youtube.com/watch?v=2mccKiZ9AfE

61. In *The Bridge at the End of the World: Capitalism, the Environment and Crossing from Crisis to Sustainability (2008)* author Professor James Gustave Speth blames the failure to halt environmental deterioration on the economic and political systems of modern capitalism. He believes we have to change the destructive operating systems of the world economy.

62. The Brundtland Commission was established by the UN to address the degradation of the environment and natural resources. Their report, *Our Common Future* (1987), was intended to rally countries to work and pursue sustainable development together.

63. Bill Gates believes that 'our food system is ripe for innovation' and that protein, derived from plants, should be developed as an alternative to meat.

64. Robert Goodland has been calculating the true impact on the planet of intensive cattle farming. Watch him on Youtube: http://www.youtube.com/watch?v=26gx-Ut_fzo

65. Vandana Shiva, Indian philosopher, environmental activist and author of *Biopiracy: The Plunder of Nature and Knowledge*. Watch her on YouTube: http://www.youtube.com/watch?v=4sUvCaHOg8Y

66. Jonathon Porritt is an environmentalist, campaigner and advocate for the Green Party of England and Wales. Watch him on YouTube:

- http://www.youtube.com/watch?v=39bPjnFBt-o

- http://www.youtube.com/watch?v=Qbl73hCCvTU

67. Kumi Naidoo, the International Executive Director of Greenpeace, is an inspiring speaker on climate change and environmental issues. Watch him on YouTube: http://www.youtube.com/watch?v=cBThSuuwLMM

Ten agencies driving change

68. The United Nations (UN) (http://www.un.org) 'is an international organisation founded in 1945… committed to maintaining international peace and security, developing friendly relations among nations and promoting social progress, better living standards and human rights.'

69. The World Health Organization (WHO) (http://www.who. Int) '…coordinating authority for health within the United Nations system. It is responsible for providing leadership on global health matters, shaping the health research agenda, setting norms and standards…'

70. UNHabitat (http://www.unhabitat.org) is the United Nations human settlements programme. It is mandated '… to promote socially and environmentally sustainable towns and cities with the goal of providing adequate shelter for all.'

71. Friends of the Earth (http://foe.co.uk) campaigns for environmental sustainability.

72. Greenpeace (http://www.greenpeace.org.uk): 'We defend the natural world and promote peace by investigating, exposing and confronting environmental abuse, and championing environmentally responsible solutions.'

73. **The Tyndall Centre for Climate Change Research** is researching climate-change issues. Dr Alice Bows-Larkin and Professor Kevin Anderson, at the Climate Change Conference in Warsaw, 2013, claimed that the only solution to climate change is for the world to consume less.

   ▶ http://www.democracynow.org/2013/11/21/we_have_to_consume_less_scientists.

74. **The World Resources Institute** is a global research organization that aims to sustain a healthy environment; the foundation of economic opportunity and human well-being.

75. **The Lincoln Institute of Land Policy,** in Cambridge, Massachusetts, is a think tank seeking to inform decision-making and influence land policy.

76. **The Academy of Urbanism** is an independent organization involved in the social, cultural, economic, political and physical development of our villages, towns and cities.

77. **The Urban Design Group (UDG)** campaigns for raising standards of urban design.

Four examples of cities in literature and films

78. *Invisible Cities* by Italo Calvino (1972) is a book set around imaginary conversations between Marco Polo and his host, the Chinese ruler Kublai Khan, which conjures up cities of magical times.

79. *Metropolis* by Fritz Lang (1927) is a milestone silent movie epic of German Expressionism. It sets out a bleak view of life and class struggle in a futuristic megacity, born out two differing visions of Germany; its mediaeval past and a modernist industrial Utopia.

80. *Escape from New York* (1981) is an American sci-fi action film by John Carpenter set in the then near-future (1997) on Manhattan Island, which has been converted into a maximum security prison.

81. *Blade Runner* (1982) is Ridley Scott's sci-fi thriller and dystopian view, vaguely based on Philip K. Dick's novel *Do Androids Dream of Electric Sheep?* It is a brilliant film even though its future vision is utterly depressing.

Five great megaproject jaw-droppers, disasters and successes

82. **Maglev high-speed trains,** using magnets to lift the train above the track, may become the future of transport links between cities. Japan is developing one that would link Tokyo to Nagoya by 2027 and Osaka by 2045 and will travel at 311 mph. Shanghai was the first city to have a commercial service in 2004 from the international airport to the city centre, but due to the short journey it only reaches a maximum speed of 268 mph.

83. **Crossrail,** London's rail project due to open in 2018, is probably one of the slowest megaprojects to get underway. The idea was first mooted in the 1930s, adopted as policy in the 1940s, but the 'Beeching cuts' to railways in the 1960s stalled it. It was revived in 1989, but the Bill submitted in 1991 failed. In 2000 the process was revived again and the scheme received consent in 2008. When it is complete it will arguably have taken about 90 years to deliver and will have cost £16 billion to build.

84. **The Boston Central Artery and Tunnel or 'Big Dig'** took 25 years from the planning phase in 1982 to completion in 2007. It removed an elevated highway and put it in a tunnel and created a new linear park. It was fraught with problems; a post-completion ceiling collapse killed a motorist and the guardrails have resulted in eight deaths to motorcyclists. It ran massively over budget, $24.3 billion from the original estimate $3 billion in 1991.

85. **London's Emirates Cable Car** is a classic example of a project with no business case. It has little justification; it goes pretty much from nowhere to nowhere, destinations are already connected by the Underground and has very low capacity. Its cost/benefit ratio does not stack up and it would never have happened, had it not been privately funded and had mayor Boris Johnson's backing. The cost was about £60 million.

86. **The London Overground service** was introduced to address a travel need that had been identified some decades earlier; the need for an orbital link within the city. With comparatively small engineering changes to existing rail infrastructure, new trains and station enhancements, a new travel option has been created that now carries 3 million passengers per week, for relatively low capital investment.

Nine cities of fantasy, myth and fiction

87. **The Tower of Babel** appears early in the Bible in Genesis 11: 1-9. A people, speaking a common language, decided to build a city 'whose top may reach unto heaven'. It is thought the Tower of Babel was the seven-stage ziggurat with a temple to the god Marduk, built in the city of Babylon in the sixth or seventh century BCE.

88. **Sodom and Gomorrah** were two cities mentioned in the Old Testament as well as in the New Testament, the Qur'an and other texts. They are believed to have been situated on the river Jordan and were destroyed by God. They are metaphors for vice and deviation.

89. **Is Atlantis a fictional city?** It was first mentioned by Plato in about 360 BCE. Apparently, after a failed attempt to invade Athens, Atlantis sank into the ocean 'in a single day and night of misfortune'.

90. **El Dorado,** a mythical city of the legendary Muisca tribal king who covered himself in gold and dived into Lake Guatavita; it became an obsessive search for the Spanish Conquistadors.

91. **The Lost City of Z** in Brazil was apparently visited by a Portuguese explorer in 1753. Despite a detailed description there was no location, and it has not yet been positively identified.

92. **Utopia** was coined by Sir Thomas More in his book of that name, from Greek rootso οὐ (not) and τόπος (place) i.e. 'no place'. You might be forgiven in thinking it should have been called 'good place' or Eutopia from Greek εν (εὖ) (good) and τόπος.

93. **Gotham City** was the home of Batman in the comic books of the 1940s. Writer and artist Frank Miller wrote 'Metropolis is New York in the daytime; Gotham City is New York at night'.

94. **Cedric Price,** twentieth-century British architect and thinker, outlined the evolution of the city in three simple drawings of an egg. The boiled egg was the ancient cities with dense compact centres protected by defensive walls. The fried egg was the cities of the seventeeth to

nineteenth centuries, once cannon-power had rendered the walls obsolete. The 'modern' city was a scrambled egg, where the core of the city has collapsed under the weight of its sprawl.

95. **British architect Ron Heron,** who was part of the avant-garde British architectural group Archigram in the 1960s, proposed a Walking City. They would be massive robotic structures that could roam the world and could lock together to form walking megalopolises. The drawings have inspired many architects.

Three urban myths

96. **In New York** in the 1930s the sewers were infested with huge alligators; the result of baby alligators being flushed down the toilet when they got to be too big to be cuddly.

97. **The entire global population** could stand shoulder to shoulder on the Isle of Wight. The Isle of Wight is 380 km². If you assume each adult occupies on average 0.5 m² and a child 0.25 m² then they would take up over 3 billion m².

98. **You are never more than six feet from a rat.** The BBC More or Less team did a calculation that there are about 3.1 million rats in the UK urban areas, which on average equates to each rat occupying 5000 m², meaning that you would typically be 50 m from one.

Two proverbs and quotations

99. Almost everyone knows Samuel Johnson's 'Why, Sir, you find no man, at all intellectual, who is willing to leave London. No, Sir, when a man is tired of London, he is tired of life; for there is in London all that life can afford.' Andy Warhol had a view of Los Angeles, but it says more about him than about the city: 'I love Los Angeles. I love Hollywood. They're beautiful. Everybody's plastic. I want to be plastic.'

100. 'You can close the city gates but not the mouths of men.' Persian proverb.

Abbreviations

BRT: Bus Rapid Transit

CHP: Combined Heat and Power

FAO: UN Food and Agriculture Organisation

GDP: Gross Domestic Product

ILWRM: Integrated Land and Water Resource Management

IPCC: Intergovernmental Panel on Climate Change

IRBM: Integrated River Basin Management

ITS: Intelligent Transport Systems

OECD: Organisation for Economic Co-operation and Development

NGO: Non-governmental Organization

Notes

Introduction

1 Rose, Eddie, *The World Population Explosion* (Yale: New Haven Teachers' Institute, 1988)

2 UNPD, *World Urbanization Prospects, the 2011* Revisions (2011)

3 Dorling, Danny, *Population 10 Billion – The Coming Demographic Crisis and How to Avoid it* (Constable 2013)

4 Cox, Wendell, *World Urban Areas Population and Density: A 2012 Update* (New Geography, 2012)

5 Geddes, Patrick, *Cities in Evolution* (1915); Mumford, Lewis, *The Culture of Cities* (1938); Gottmann, Jean, *Megalopolis. The Urbanized Northeastern seaboard of the United States* (1961).

6 UN Habitat, World Urbanization Prospects, the 2011 Revisions (March 2012)

7 *UN World Urbanization Prospects, the 2011 Revisions.*

8 *UN World Urbanization Prospects, the 2005 Revisions.*

9 *Metropolises and Sustainability*: The UCL Environment Institute Seminar Series Report 2009.

10 UN *World Urbanization Prospects, the 2011 Revisions.*

11 Johnson, Ian, *New York Times* (15 June 2013).

Chapter 1

12 UN Habitat, *Hot Cities: the Battle-ground for Climate Change* (2011).

13 WHO/UNICEF JMP, *Progress on Sanitation and Drinking-Water: Update 2010* (2010).

14 UN Habitat, *Urban Development and Management* (November 2013)

15 International Energy Agency (2006).

16 Department for Transport, *Roads: Delivering choice and reliability* (2008).

ALL THAT MATTERS: FUTURE CITIES

17 WHO, *Global Age-friendly Cities: A Guide* (2007).

18 Sootfree for the Climate, *City Ranking* (2011).

19 IOM, *Report on estimation of mortality impacts of particulate air pollution in London* (2010).

20 Environment Agency website www.environment-agency.gov.uk/ (acessed February 2014)

Chapter 2

21 UNEP (2011).

22 Wang, Edward, *New York Times* (1 June 2011).

23 National Geographic (www.nationalgeographic.com), *The Global Water Footprint of Key Crops* (accessed March 2014).

Chapter 3

24 Hansen, James, *Storms of My Grandchildren: The Truth About the Coming Climate Catastrophe and Our Last Chance to Save Humanity* (Bloomsbury, 2009).

25 Greenpeace, *Decentralising Energy: Cleaner, Cheaper, more Secure energy for 21st Century Britain* (March 2006)

26 Presentation at the Independent Transport commission Annual Lecture 2013; Fusion: Feasibility and the Future of Transport

Chapter 4

27 'Everyone has the right to a standard of living adequate for the health and well-being of himself and of his family, including food, clothing, housing and medical care and necessary social services, and the right to security in the event of unemployment, sickness, disability, widowhood, old age or other lack of livelihood in circumstances beyond his control.' UN Declaration of Human Rights (Article 25-1).

28 www.affordablehousinginstitute.org/ resources/features/

29 GLA Intelligence Unit (2011); World Urban Areas Population and Density: 2012 Update.

Chapter 5

30 International Transport Forum, OECD, *Reducing Transport Greenhouse Gas Emissions* (2010).

31 Litman, Todd, *Transportation Land Valuation* (Victoria Transport Policy Institute, 2012)

32 *International Journal of SustainableTransportation* Vol 5, No 1 (2011).

Chapter 6

33 BBC Shared Planet (9 September 2013).

34 Goodland, Robert, talk at Gwangju Summit of Urban Environment, 'Accords: Food and Climate Change: Risk and Opportunity for Korea and the World' (2011)

35 UN FAO, 'Livestock's Long Shadow', *Environmental Issues and Options* (2006).

36 http://supremastertv.com/pe/?wr_id=166

37 BBC Radio 4, Shared Planet (9 September 2013)

Chapter 7

38 Loukaitou-Sideris, Anastasia, *Urban parks*, UCL Institute for Environment and Sustainability (2006).

Chapter 8

39 Formally known as the World Commission on Environment and Development (WCED), the Brundtland Commission was established by the UN. At the time it was recognized that free markets and global activity were causing heavy degradation of the human environment and natural resources. *Our Common Future* was intended to rally countries to work and pursue sustainable development together.

40 Goodland, Robert, 'The Concept of Environmental Sustainability, *Annual Review of Ecology and Systmatics*, Volume 26 (1995) 1-24

41 Dorling, Danny, *Population 10 Billion – The Coming Demographic Crisis and How to Survive it* (Constable, 2013).

42 'Making Data Dance', *Economist Technology Quarterly* (Q4 2010)

43 By consultants Best Foot Forward.

44 Forbes (Washington,16 April 2013).

45 London Councils website (www.londoncouncils.gov.uk) (accessed March 2014).

46 USA Census Bureau.

47 Water Footprint Network.

48 Nature Communications 4, Article number 2934 doi: 10.1038/ncommms3934)

49 Hansard (2 July 1986).

50 The Housing Unit, *Regular Report on Housing Developments in European Countries* (2004).

51 UN HABITAT, *State of the world's cities 2006/7*

Conclusion

52 Popper, Karl, *The Myth of the Framework* (Routledge, 1994).

Acknowledgements

I want to thank Zoe Goldstein for her enlightened editorial suggestions and for unravelling my inconsitencies and ambiguities.

Picture credits

The authors and publisher would like to give their thanks for permission to reproduce the following images:

Introduction Map showing percentage of world population in urban areas taken from United Nations, Department of Economic and Social Affairs, Population Division: World Population Prospects Demobase extract © 2007

Chapter 1 London Heat Map © Mayor of London and the London Heat Map

Chapter 3 Conventional energy generation and transmission © Greenpeace/breeze; Landfill site © Shutterstock.com

Chapter 4 Slums © Aleksander Todorovic/Shutterstock.com & Brian S/Shutterstock.com; UN slum map adapted from the UN Millenniums Project © 2005

Index

Note: City names are listed by their country, e.g. 'Greece (Athens)', except for 'London, UK', which is filed as a separate entry.

ALL THAT MATTERS: FUTURE CITIES

ALL THAT MATTERS: FUTURE CITIES